Finding The Authentic You

Your destiny is discovering YOU

LAINIE MORRISON-FRYER

BALBOA.PRESS
A DIVISION OF HAY HOUSE

Balboa Press books may be ordered through booksellers or by contacting:

Balboa Press
A Division of Hay House
1663 Liberty Drive
Bloomington, IN 47403
www.balboapress.com
844-682-1282

Because of the dynamic nature of the Internet, any web addresses or links contained in this book may have changed since publication and may no longer be valid. The views expressed in this work are solely those of the author and do not necessarily reflect the views of the publisher, and the publisher hereby disclaims any responsibility for them.

The author of this book does not dispense medical advice or prescribe the use of any technique as a form of treatment for physical, emotional, or medical problems without the advice of a physician, either directly or indirectly. The intent of the author is only to offer information of a general nature to help you in your quest for emotional and spiritual well-being. In the event you use any of the information in this book for yourself, which is your constitutional right, the author and the publisher assume no responsibility for your actions.

Author Photo by Sue Burke

Scripture quotations marked NIV are taken from the Holy Bible, New International Version®. NIV®. Copyright © 1973, 1978, 1984 by International Bible Society. Used by permission of Zondervan. All rights reserved. [Biblica]

Print information available on the last page.

ISBN: 978-1-9822-6555-7 (sc)
ISBN: 978-1-9822-6554-0 (hc)
ISBN: 978-1-9822-6553-3 (e)

Library of Congress Control Number: 2021904768

Balboa Press rev. date: 05/20/2021

To my children:
Natalie Marguerite
Grant Steven
Ava Elaine
Jackson Reece
Marco Atilio
Ana Francis

You are my love, my light, and my purpose.
Never forget how important you are!

ACKNOWLEDGMENTS

Thank you to my amazing, loving, and supportive husband, Matthew. Special thanks to my mom Sandy, my mother-in-law Marilynn and grandmother Sharon and my soul tribe sisters and those of you who have left your print on my soul: Jennifer T., Marie, Nicole, Marlene, Maricel, Angie, Meribah, Tracy, Susan, Tracey, Tammy, Lisa, Yvonne, Lynn, Candace, Julie, Patty, Brenda, Vicky, Tiffany, Christie, Lynne, Sylvia, Theresa, Marnie, Kim, Mary, Vickie, Jackie, Heather, Bethe, Lenda, Julie, Dena, Trish, Lori, Shannon, Shirley, Pam, Christie, Janine, and my dance mamas: Debby, Lynne, Mena, Vina, Melissa, Pam, Lisa, Andrea, Cara, Jackie, Julie, Kristen, Amy, and many more from my years as a dance mom and teacher at Children's Dance Theater, Dance Athletics Competitive Edge, and Big City Dance Center. I also must mention all my Mary Kay girlfriends: Margaret, Lisa, Jennifer, Debbie, and my entire M.K. Unit. Your love, light, and friendships mean the world to me.

CONTENTS

PART 6: FINAL WORDS

INTRODUCTION

Photographed by Ava E. Morrison

The Beginning

On June 11, 2015, after battling both lung and pancreatic cancer for many years, my dad, Richard Turner Sr., died. He was my "balcony" person—the one who cheered me on from the moment I entered this world. To describe him in one word, a sentence, or even a paragraph would never do him justice or even come close to explaining the positive impact he had not only on me but on everyone he encountered. This book was inspired by the beautiful tapestry that my dad wove over his sixty-eight years of life. He created his masterpiece not through his final bow but through each minute, year, and decade of discovering his authentic self and living it. This book describes how his journey wove into my journey and how it influenced the choices I have made in the discovery of my true authentic self.

One of the lessons that my amazing father taught me was the gift of writing. He was an extremely artistically talented, self-taught musician and songwriter. He taught me the value of giving a hard day's work. He also taught me, through his actions and not his words, that spending time with people and sharing in their joy and happiness is one of the greatest gifts that we as humans can give to one another. I always tell my children that we are not here to compete with one another, but we are here to complete one another. As my father was entering his last few months of life, I asked him to write letters to each of his grandchildren. He was too sick to write himself, so, as he laid in the hospital bed in my parents' family room, where he spent his last months of life, he dictated those letters to me as I typed. I honestly did not realize the impact and importance of this moment or the eternal footprint his letters would have on us all until much later. I am grateful that I followed through on the prompting to ask him to write and even more thankful that he agreed to do so. My children, niece, and nephew cherish these letters from my father. As Benjamin Franklin once said, "If you would not be forgotten as soon as you are dead and rotten, either write something worth reading or do something worth writing."[1] My dad did both.

---

[1] Benjamin Franklin, *Poor Richard's Almanack* (Philadelphia: Benjamin Franklin, 1732).

As parents, we strive to do our absolute best, but often we fall short. Sometimes our failures are not seen by others, only felt within the privacy of our own hearts. Other times, our failures are felt by our children, and they bear the responsibility of making the decision to either use those mistakes as lessons or to use those mistakes as excuses for negative choices they make in their own lives. Some of our parental failures are seen by the naked eye of those who may choose to watch quietly on the sidelines of life or by others that may interject their opinions. Whatever category our mistakes fall into, they leave us parents questioning our childrearing abilities. If you have felt this feeling, you are not alone. You are a great parent! The key is to never stop learning, improving who you are, or sharing your love, gifts, and talents with not only your children but everyone you meet.

Over five years have passed since my father's death, and I still think of him daily and feel his presence in my everyday life. What has gotten me through the grief, hurt, bitterness, anger, frustration, and the simple feeling of just wanting to have him back has been the love from God, my family, and friends. Three of my "lifer" girlfriends, Marie, Jennifer, and Nicole, were the driving force behind my journey of completing and publishing this book. I would like to tell you a little bit about them, how our universes collided, and what brought us together to share our lives, knowledge, mistakes, laughter, and faith, all of which launched me on the journey of writing this book.

My Soul Tribe

Marie

I am starting with Marie because I met her first. While attending a local university, I took on the role as an administrative assistant for an organization in order to financially support myself. The organization offered various educational courses and seminars for misdemeanor defendants who committed crimes such as drunk driving, possession of illegal substances, domestic abuse, economic crime, and various driving-related offenses. After

I had been working there three years, the organization hired Marie to run our youthful offender program. I immediately fell in love with her. She is the youngest of twelve children, so you can imagine her wit and great sense of humor. Her positive energy, love of life, and unwavering faith are some of the many attributes I love best about her. We were roommates for about a year, and I will share those stories another time. As the years passed, we moved on to different jobs, got married, and had kids. We did our best to remain connected, but for many years when our kids were little, we spoke only every few months. Despite the distance of time, our connection was so strong that we never allowed it to affect our lifelong friendship. If anything, it made us realize how important we were to each other and how our lives would forever be woven together. Marie is a social worker and educational specialist with a Licensed Master Social Worker, (LMSA), Educational Specialist Degree, (Ed.S.).[2] She runs her own business offering counseling and educational services for both adult and juvenile clients.

Jennifer

Jennifer and I met while I was working at the same organization as above, but our friendship truly began when I took my second "real" job working as a court reporter at a local court where Jennifer was also employed. We worked together there for ten years, and through typical work drama, getting married, and having kids, our bond only grew closer. We too have remained in contact over the years, sharing our happiness, joy, sorrow, grief, frustrations of marriage, and raising children. Like Marie, she comes from an exceptionally large family. We are all the "babies" of our families. What I love about Jennifer is her free-spirited nature, her laughter, and her faith. Jennifer has a love and light for the world that are more influential than she'll ever know. She has an innate ability to speak truth into others with such grace and dignity. Her graceful directness is such a blessing. I hope that our journey together affords her the opportunity to gain greater awareness and personal acknowledgment of her gifts and talents. On our

---

[2] "Meet the Staff," Journey of Hope, accessed October 30, 2020, www.journeyofhopeservices.com.

parallel spiritual journeys, Jennifer and I both achieved our certifications as Master Reiki Practitioners, and in 2020 we began our own company.[3]

We all turned fifty the year I began this book. I'm not certain if it was the stars aligning, divine intervention, or honestly the fact that we are all now a half century old, but we all felt this uncontrollable, uncontainable, burst of excitement and drive to do more, be more, and give more. Of course, we did not know what exactly that would entail, which brings me to how this book was born.

One of my former neighbors, Angie, opened her own business specializing in holistic occupational therapy, pulse magnetic practices, and Holy Fire Reiki.[4] Jennifer and I, along with some other girlfriends, decided to attend one of her sessions. There were five of us lying on mats in a small room, so close that our bodies nearly touched one another. The energy in the room that night was magical, spiritual, magnetic, healing, and so influential. After leaving the session, Jennifer and I felt even more connected and convicted that we needed to begin a joint venture together.

About two weeks later, I met with Marie for dinner. The conversation quickly turned to faith and spirituality, our life purpose, and an almost desperate desire to do more, give more, and be more. That is when it all came together. I shared with Marie that I wanted to write a memoir for my six children. I told her that I wanted to title it *What I Know at Fifty That I Wish I Knew at Twenty*. Instead of laughing at my idea, as I thought she might, she reached across the table, grabbed my hands, and said, "Do this for your children." The excitement within my heart pumped through my veins, and I started talking about a thousand miles a minute.

Nicole

As I started this journey, I realized that my other important human link was my beautiful sister-in-law Nicole. Have you ever met a person whom you know you have met before? The first time we met, I had that feeling

---

[3] www.mindfulblissliving.com.
[4] www.soulscapewellnesshaven.com.

of familiarity and comfort and such a powerful connection that I really could not describe it. The crazy thing is that she felt it too. We always joked that we were sisters in a past life. Maybe we were. She and my brother-in-law started their marriage in Michigan, but due to career changes, they moved to Oklahoma and then eventually settled in Florida. Despite the miles between our families, we make a conscious effort to stay connected. Throughout the past ten-plus years, we have noticed the serendipities of our spiritual journeys. Over the past year, it became obvious to us both that our journeys were meant to be linked together. Like parallel lines that twist together to create a stronger cord, our lives have done the same. The thicker the cord, the stronger it is. Basically, she gives me strength. Like my brother-in-law says, we are all unique individuals, like "special snowflakes." Nicole is a Ho'Oponopono advanced practitioner.[5]

Spiritual gifts are different from person to person. I love it that the strengths of Jennifer, Marie, and Nicole are my weaknesses, and my strengths are their weaknesses. We complete one another.

Nicole is the second of four daughters with an Italian father and Polish mother. She is passionate, loving, caring, smart, and beautiful. She is the most amazing mother to three beautiful sons and one beautiful daughter. I am so grateful for her love, light, wisdom, and guidance.

I believe that Marie gave me the strength to begin this book, and Jennifer and Nicole helped me complete it. I am forever grateful for the daily blessings that these three amazing women bring to my life.

"The cord of three strands is not quickly broken" (Ecclesiastes 4:12). And so it begins.

The Title of This Book

The title was originally *What I Know at Fifty That I Wish I Knew at Twenty.* I did not intend that title to mean that readers had to be under fifty to

---

[5] landhealing.com.

read the book, nor did it mean that they had to be over twenty. I liked the initial title because, in my own life and personal experiences prior to age twenty, I was not ready to receive the truths that life had to offer. I think about myself as a child and a teen, when my elders were trying to share some wisdom and some monumental story in their attempt to help me figure out a problem, concern, or disappointment in my own life, I was not ready for that lesson. Most of the time, I really was not mature enough to hear the story, let alone understand the meaning behind it. As I got older, I realized the importance of sitting and listening—really listening—to my dad, my mom, my grandparents, and my elders because, honestly, they had a lot of great stuff to share! As I got older, I realized that I was mature enough to listen to their stories and wise enough to apply those lessons to my own life. I also realized that in my own life's journey, the resulting lessons that I will share with you on the following pages, have unfolded in their own unique time. As I was completing the book, I turned fifty-two years old and realized that the title needed to be changed. So I opted for *Finding the Authentic You.*

The knowledge, wisdom, and life experiences we achieve through a half century of walking on this earth can fill up the pages of this book and all the shelves in a library. I hope that the few stories, lessons, and life journeys, I share with you now, help you navigate through the potholes or bumps in the road as you journey through your own life destiny. It is my wish for you, the reader, that you can see the simple truths to the stories and statements that have poured out of my heart, soul, and mind. I pray that the chapters, paragraphs, statements, and words not only resonate with you but stir your own soul so much that you take a deeper look within yourself. I hope that it moves you into action to achieve the absolute best life for yourself in this lifetime. It is a lifetime that was designed for you, even before you were born, because you actually chose it. I hope that you enjoy the journey of *Finding the Authentic You.*

This book was originally written for my children, all six of them—products of a blended family. We are a modern-day Brady Bunch, so to speak, minus Alice and Sam the butcher! When I began to write this book, my kids' ages ranged from fourteen to twenty-three; as I complete it, they are from sixteen to twenty-five. I wanted to leave them just a small piece of me that each of them could hold onto, other than a photo or keepsake. I wanted to give them a gift of my words of love, faith, joy, happiness, sorrow, struggles, and ultimately the wisdom I've learned in my life, with the hopes that it might be a beacon of light in times of darkness in their own lives.

When I shared my idea with my oldest daughter, Natalie, she suggested a specific sequence for the book—the chronological order of my life. I thought about it, but as I started to write, I realized that the majority of these life lessons did not come at any specific moment in my life. They were learned from all my collective experiences. They were like building blocks, connecting with one another at different moments in my life. The lessons that I learned were not in black and white. They were more like the smears of colors found in broken color-painting techniques used by many insurgent artists, unabashed brushstrokes to blend the colors together, creating the light of life. So I hope you can follow along as I meander through the lessons I learned in my journey of life on my own road in finding my true self. I hope that these stories put a smile on your face, make you laugh out loud, make you shed a tear, or make your heart skip a beat, and I hope that this book leaves you with a warm, full heart for the love, beauty, and joy of your own life. Let your soul resonate and your spirit ascend as you read through the pages of my personal life experiences and uncover the secrets of living the life you want and deserve.

PART 1

Our Existence

Photographer: Kerman Delaiso,
Master Photographer of Oddusee Photography

CHAPTER 1

The Truth about You

You have a soul, which you can think of as your consistent, and you have a personality, which you can think of as the product of your DNA; your environment; and your astrological makeup, which includes your birth chart, your life purpose number, and your destiny number, in addition to your enneagram.[6] All these components, like the ingredients used to make a cake, are then topped with the colorful sprinkles of your own unique life experiences. Wow, that is a lot. It is no wonder that we are all so uniquely different. The truth is that many other factors are woven into the makeup of your authentic soul. Many of us want to blame the negative experiences from our childhood for who we are today. I absolutely despise it when I hear people use the excuse, "Well, it's just who I am" or "I'm only human." Really? But we are all so much more, and therefore I disagree with those excuses. I stand firm on the truth that our childhoods are the foundations of the types of people we become in our human earth avatars, but just like a huge skyscraper, the foundation is just the beginning. The two parts of our human avatars consist of our soul and our character. The soul is unchanging, yet it can grow through each soul contract and is therefore the foundation of our consciousness, yet our character is pliable and is, therefore, the building blocks. The building blocks assist our souls on the journey of discovering our authentic selves.

---

[6] Alex Fletcher, *Astrology and Enneagram* (New York, New York, Alex Fletcher, November 2018).

What were the first few blocks on your foundation? Did you have a pleasant childhood filled with unconditional love and support in a genuinely happy household? Or was your childhood filled with conditional love? Was your household a place of peace, a haven in times of trouble, or was your house filled with anger, a battlefield that you wanted to escape? Were you raised by two parents or by a single parent? Maybe you were not even raised by your parents. Regardless of your childhood environment, those experiences do not define the person you are today; they are the first few building blocks of who you are at this very moment. To understand the first layer of blocks in your foundational structure, you need to ask yourself what kind of person you were in childhood.

Were you a people pleaser, as I used to be? Perhaps your parents bragged about you and compared your siblings to you to the point that you knew that, if you did not meet their expectations, your whole world and existence would explode like an erupting volcano. This potential eruption felt as if it could destroy you and those around you. Being raised as a people pleaser is tough because you are more concerned about other people's happiness than about focusing on finding and discovering your own happiness. As a people pleaser, you also allow other people's opinions of you to define who you are. Even if you are a confident person, you find that you still second-guess yourself all the time. You feel as if your self-worth is wrapped up in how happy you make others feel, and the consequence of such thinking is mentally damaging. When those people are not happy, you feel as if you obviously did not do your job. I lived many years carrying around this heavy, cumbersome title. I did not even realize that I was one until one day I woke up and felt unfulfilled and unhappy. I was sick and tired of being in situations that I knew in my gut I did not want to be part of, yet I felt obligated to say yes. In those moments, I felt my inner three-year-old throw herself onto the floor and have a full-blown tantrum—screaming and flailing my arms and legs, while saying to myself, *I don't want to be here. This is not what I want to be doing right now.* A wise woman once told me, "When you say yes to something that wasn't ever meant for you, you are taking away that opportunity from someone else." Wow—so simple, yet so profound. It took me what felt like forever not only to learn this lesson but to implement it in my daily life. Because of my personality, I still find myself being drawn into situations where I almost say yes, and I must be mindful in order to catch the yes and turn it into a no. After I decline the opportunity, I feel a huge burden lifted off my shoulders, and I can breathe more easily because it was not what I was meant to do.

The second lesson here for all you people pleasers is that you do not have to give an explanation to back up or support your no. Just say no or no thank you. Why do we feel the need to back up every choice we make with an explanation? It's likely because we are not doing what the other person wants us to do, but it is not that person's life. It is your life.

Maybe you were the rebel of the family—the one who felt as if you were expected to always push the envelope, so you did. You did what you wanted to without any care about the effects your actions had on yourself and others. Sometimes your actions led to self-sabotage, and other times they hurt others. As the rebel of the family, sometimes you do these things for attention, and it does not really matter if it is good or bad attention. You just need to get attention. Maybe you were just trying to find your own voice and express your independence in your attempt to find your true self. You were not afraid to explore all that life has to offer, even if it involved risky behavior. The rebel of the family is a tough role to play because sometimes you find yourself in situations that you cannot dig your way out of. You need to find a balance between being a risk-taker and finding adventure without putting yourself or others in danger. Others may get the impression that you care only about yourself, but that is not true. You have a lot of love for others, but it gets masked by your flippant attitude or your I-do-not-care actions. If you are the rebel, remember that your family and friends are not trying to control you; they are just trying to keep you safe. You can still have adventure and excitement in your life without putting yourself in potentially dangerous situations.

Maybe you were the quiet one—the one who did not need much attention while growing up. You enjoyed living life under the radar because the thought of being seen or heard put you into such a tailspin of panic that you would rather hide under a rock than be noticed. You enjoy time alone or with your close, intimate group of friends. Large gatherings make you feel extremely uncomfortable, and you want to crawl out of your skin when put in this situation. You were an easy child to raise because even your worst tantrums were mild in comparison to those of your siblings. You rarely talked back to your parents and were a very obedient student. You were so obedient that sometimes it was like you were not even there because you loved to blend into the tapestry of life. People assumed that there was not much to your personality, but they were so wrong. There is a lot brewing under the quiet surface. You are an observer of people, places, and situations. You take in more than others see. You might even be an empath. If you are, then you need to take time away from others to reground yourself. Because of this, being in crowds of people becomes overwhelming for you because of the heightened emotional energies that only an empath, like you, can feel. If you are a quiet one, embrace the specialness of who you are. You are a gift.

Maybe you were the life of the party—the one who captivated the audience the moment you entered this world. You oozed so much charm and charisma that things just seemed to come naturally easier for you than others. When you enter a room, your vivacious personality and charisma draw all eyes to you. Those around you are drawn to your high energy level. People with lower energy levels are drawn toward your light. They want to be a part of that higher frequency that you so naturally project onto those around you. You may not even realize that you are this person; you just know that you love being around other people. You tend to make others feel better about themselves, and when you leave their space, they still do. You can make others feel lighter and happier. Your positive energy overflows out of you and sprinkles over others. That is why other people absolutely love to have you around. This is a gift; you have no idea! Keep spreading your love and light. You may unintentionally overshadow others because of your strong presence. You will be successful in any career involving interaction with others, but be cautious of the energy vampires who will try to steal your high-vibe energy and light. You will also need to take time away to ground yourself and recharge with other high-vibe people.

Maybe you were the comedian of the family—the one who could make people laugh in those serious moments. At family and friend gatherings, you are the one who is in the center of the circles as you share your stories, which bring roars of laughter from the crowds. You do have a serious side, but most people see only your lighthearted side because this is who you are, and this is what you want them to see. You share your serious side only with those closest to you. Your tribe sees this side of you but only when you want them to. You not only have a gift of humor, but you are also a gift because in those serious moments and in the darkest hours of life, you can make dire situations feel lighter. You can lift the burden and sadness of others by your humor. Keep sharing the humor and bringing laughter into the world.

Maybe you were the Sarcastic one - the one who would respond with one-liners that sometimes were so brassy or raw that they teetered on offensive, yet a sliver of truth in your brassiness made others laugh, or maybe made only you laugh. You are quick-witted and you see the realness of situations and things. You bring your humor alive with your sarcasm. When you were younger, usually only older kids or adults got your humor. You find joy in making others laugh, but you have less respect for those who do not get your level of humor. There are times when you offend others with your sarcasm, which sometimes is your initial intent. You need to be careful because your words sting others, even if that is not your intention. You are a realist in the family, and you can cut through the crap and fluff and get right to the core of any situation with your directness.

Maybe you were the Winnie-the-Pooh of the family—the person for whom life was and still may be simple. Your main concern was getting that darn honey out of the pot, taking a nice long nap, and having fun with your friends. You are fun-loving, sweet, and caring, and you are content with your spot in life. You rarely compare yourself to others or make judgments of them. You are content with who you are, and you respect people for where they are in their own lives. You know how to have fun, and you treasure your friends and family. You are loyal and honest and are a great friend. The inner child in you is still extraordinarily strong, and you easily find joy in life's little blessings. You sometimes live in your own fantasy world and need to be more aware of the realities of life. You may be taken advantage of by others because of your naïve nature.

Maybe you were the intense one—the one who felt and loved things so deeply that sometimes your intensity was too much for others around you. Your level of connection and deep feelings for other people, places, and things are more concentrated than they are for others. You love deeply and can despise equally deeply. You give 100 percent of yourself to what you believe in because, for you, there is no other way to commit. Due to your intense nature, you have empathic characteristics just like the quiet one, and therefore you may feel overwhelmed in large crowds. You are a great listener, and you can immerse yourself deeply in a person, activity, or interest. You can be deeply passionate, yet you may find yourself to be very possessive or jealous due to your intense nature. You also may obsess over things due to your extreme emotions.

Maybe you were the creative one—the one who could quietly lose yourself in your artistry while creating some amazing masterpieces that would take others a lifetime to create. Your love and connection to your talent not only provided you with an escape from life's reality but also afforded you the ability to tap into your true voice. As a creative one, you tend to be alone more than others because that is when you can truly tap into the core of your artistic nature. You may be a bit quirky or odd, but it is your uniqueness that allows the exposure of your raw, creative, artistic flair. Don't ever change. You are a masterpiece, but make sure you take time to spend with your loved ones. Take those blinders off for a while to capture balance in your life.

Maybe you were the free spirit—the one who that would drop whatever you were doing to go on an adventure at any given moment without a care in the world. You never take things too seriously, and you can calm chaotic crowds and situations with your mere presence and vibration of peace and love. You are envied by many because you can do whatever you love or want without getting caught up in planning or caring what others think. You do not worry too much about the effect that your choices have on others because—let's face it—it does not even cross your mind. You have many friends but not many close friends because you rarely let people get too deep with you. This is my late cousin, Brett Marihugh, who was a Navy SEAL. He was authentic to the very core. He was so real and raw and fearless. He gave his life protecting our freedom in his quest to become the absolute best he could be. He broke records while in his naval training because why not? That is just who he was. He was so charismatic that anyone near him was drawn into his colorful aura. He died a month before my aunt Doty, who was his grandmother, and two months before my dad. It was a year of losses in our family. I must believe that he is one of our guardian angels in heaven. He was fearless and reckless, lived life on the edge of existence, and would not have had it any other way. The free spirits of the world sometimes have a hard time staying in one marriage, one job, or one community because these things can feel suffocating to them. Hopefully, you can find the balance of grounding your roots yet spreading your wings to have the best of both worlds.

Maybe you were the "always right"—the one always up for a debate and sure that your point of view was the right one. You were the one who had such passion for your cause that every ounce of your being would be committed to the discussion or debate. You really do know a lot because you research things and like having this knowledge to share with others. Being always right might provide you with an air of superiority, but to those around you, it might bring annoyance. Others sometimes feel that you come across as arrogant and a know-it-all, so you need to be careful of that pitfall.

Maybe you were the golden child—the one who for some reason was believed to be the favorite. It could have been because you were the first born and your parents had so much pride in the mere fact of your birth that you achieved that supreme status. The golden child is sometimes sweet and sometimes sassy. You can play the part in any situation. Your siblings are completely annoyed with you most of the time because you get away with everything that they did not. Everything you accomplish is golden. You could not do wrong in the eyes of your parents. Falling into this category has provided you with self-confidence, but you need to remember that you may not be the golden child in the real world. This harsh reality can sometimes be a setback for you.

Maybe you were the baby of the family — the one who got whatever you wanted. Your older siblings were not only mad that your parents were way too easy on you, but they were also annoyed with you just for being the baby. Maybe you still get away with murder because of that original baby status card you pull out of your pocket when it can work in your favor. It is funny because, as the baby, you like to come in first in everything else in life. You are done with being last, unless of course you can use that status to your advantage. You learned from your older siblings and matured at a much faster rate than they did. Your confidence might take you far in life, but you may also struggle. The struggle is caused by the sense of helplessness you may carry around with you that creates a feeling of dependence on others.

Maybe you were the pitied one of the family—the one for whom people always felt bad and as if you were victimized in some way. You felt as if you got the short end of the stick all the time and never got what you deserved. You have the "woe is me" mentality and walk through life looking only at the injustices thrown at you, failing to see the blessings all around you. This can be a dangerous view to operate with in life and could lead you to a state of feeling depressed with a sense of helplessness.

Maybe you were the Pretty one — the one that from the moment you were born into this world, your beauty made the sunshine warmer, the sky bluer, and the stars brighter. You were titled as the family beauty. Your outward perfection was the only thing that you thought brought you love and attention, so much so that you make it your number one priority to never leave the house without looking your absolute best. You felt as if most people only saw your outer beauty and never really took the time to see that you also had inner beauty, so you had to work hard—harder than others—to prove to the world that you were more than just a pretty face.

Maybe you were the attention seeker—the one who always had to be the center of attention to feel as if you mattered to the world. You felt as if love for yourself came only through the attention you got from others, and therefore you worked hard to manipulate situations and others so you could be noticed, sometimes to the detriment of others. You can have quite a quick wit and sense of humor and can capture the crowds, or you can choose to gain the attention you need through poor behavior and choices in your life.

Honestly, I could go on and on with these descriptions. As you read through them, I know that you related to at least one, if not more than one, of these familiar family titles. Not only does it describe who you are, but you are also envisioning the titles that other members of your family, your friends, and your coworkers wear.

Did you notice that I tried to use the word *were* instead of *are*, past tense instead of present tense? The reason I did this is that, despite the labels that were placed on you when you were younger or the labels you gave yourself, you do not have to keep that title. You are only what you choose to be in this very moment of your life. A simple truth to life is that whatever you believe you are, you are. If you believe that you are only the label or labels you were given, then that is all you will be. If you know that you are more than that label, then you can grow into so much more—the more that your creator designed you to be. You get to decide. Remember, these are just some of the building blocks in your tower. You can move them, add to them, and change them any time that you choose.

As I said, you probably could connect to at least one label, but you are more than one label, as are most of us. These labels follow you through life and obviously have affected who you are and where you are today. But if you think for one moment that is all that you are, then you have a lot more to learn about yourself. You are an amazingly awesome gift from above. Your precious soul is a blessing to not only you, in a micro sense, but also to the entire world and universe, on a macro scale. Think large and be grand! You have specific gifts and talents that are as unique as your fingerprint, which only you possess.

Despite all that we are made of, we can choose to change, to grow, and to become all that we were made to be. So, at this very moment, if you are feeling unhappy with the label that you were given or the label you claimed for yourself, you can change it. If you like your label, you can cultivate it. If you want a different label, you can create it. You can create, define, develop, achieve, and grow into anything that you choose to be. The choice is up to you.

I believe that God does not call the equipped; He equips the called. There is a reason you were born to the parents you were born to, lived in the neighborhood you grew up in, have the friends you have, and work in the job or career that you are in right now. Is this the end? Heck, no. You are a living energy force in motion. Newton's first law of motion states, "An object at rest stays at rest, and an object in motion stays in motion with the same speed and in the same direction unless acted upon by an unbalanced force."[7] You are that *force*. You can change your speed and your direction at any point in your life, so what are you waiting for? Your foundation is the building blocks of your present and your future.

Maybe you are thinking right now, *But you don't understand because*—fill in the blank. No, I do understand, and I too am a work in progress.

Where do you start? How do you make the changes that are required to realize your full potential? You start with listening to your true, authentic self through that inner voice that whispers to you about how amazing you are. You need to ask your inner voice, "What is my purpose?" This is the first step in discovering your personal goals. I feel like so many of us do not take the time for ourselves to even find out what we really want out of life. With any personal goal, you also need a vision. How do you find your vision? You must first start with solitude, a timeout, and perhaps some meditation. You need to empty your mind of all distractions to really hear yourself, your inner voice. Spend some "self-time" without distraction to meditate, reflect, and pray. It is the best way to truly hear your inner self. Tap into the exciting wonder of your own intuition, your inner compass. I once heard that our minds are masses of emptiness that were meant to be filled with the emotions of our hearts. When you listen with your heart,

---

[7] Nancy Hall, "Newton's Laws of Motion," Glenn Research Center, accessed May 5, 2015, https://www.grc.nasa.gov/WWW/K-12/airplane/newton.html; Jon Mertz, "The Broken World Awaits You," Thin Difference, March 31, 2018, https://www.thindifference.com/2018/03/broken-world-awaits-you/.

to your true self, you will hear the positive, loving, encouraging words that can fill your mind. Do some soul searching and find the person you really are and who you were meant to be. And when you find him or her, give your higher self a huge hug of appreciation and thank your soul self for being on this journey with you.

Once you do this, you will hear a deep and clear voice within the depth of your soul telling you, *Yes, there is something more, something bigger and greater for you than you have ever imagined.* You will achieve clarity for your mission of growth and change. When you continue to take time for yourself each day, you will create a desire so raw, courageous, and fearless that nothing will stand in your way. Your passionate desire will support and sustain you on your growth journey.

Remember the little girl or boy inside of you? The one who had big, awesomely audacious goals and an unwavering vision of what you wanted out of life? Those dreams and visions were placed in your heart for a reason. Do not dismiss them, store them on the shelf with your old photo books, or bury them deep inside your treasure chest of keepsakes. The roadblocks that got in your way, keeping you from obtaining your goals, still might be the very reason you chose to forget what exactly your goals and dreams were. Do not panic and feel like past choices stopped you from achieving your dreams. You might have felt that the different path you took in life, in the opposite direction of your dreams, caused you to lose out on the opportunity of achieving your dreams and goals. I am going to tell you right now that you are far from the truth. That is a big fat lie you are telling yourself because you are afraid. I get it; fear can feel real. The acronym for fear is, "False Evidence Appearing Real." But my sweet friend, faith and fear cannot occupy the same space. Those obstacles were put there for a reason. You are on a journey of learning through your experiences, and let me tell you, God has a great sense of humor. If you do not get the lesson the first time, He will teach you repeatedly until you get it. The importance of the lesson is found in its secret. You cannot move to the next chapter or level of life until you unveil the secret of the lesson. Just like learning our ABCs or how to tie our shoes, some lessons are quickly achieved and others take lots of time. These lessons, or what you may refer to as roadblocks, helped define who you are today. There was something important in each bump you felt that now defines who you are. Those experiences created you, molded you, strengthened you, defined and refined you, and led you to the next turn on your path in discovering your true self.

So take out those goals and dreams, dust them off, shine them up and really look at them. Do not be intimidated by those roadblocks. In fact, just remove them completely from your mind and create your own new reality.

How do you change those discovered visions and dreams into goals? Your thoughts of achieving your goals need to ignite a desire—I mean a deep desire—that stirs your soul. Without a true longing for something, you will not have strength, determination, or perseverance to see it through. To break through those barriers, you need fearless commitment. How many times do we start a New Year's resolution that we feel we can commit to, yet by Valentine's Day that resolution has been long forgotten? How many times have you started and stopped something good in your life because your conviction and commitment to your goal was not strong enough to see it through to the finish line? You need to keep your vibes high and move those distant hopes, dreams, and goals closer. They need to be within your eyesight daily. You might need to make a vision board that you look at day and night. Get passionate about them and feel that fire ignite within your gut.

Once you ignite that desire, you are ready to act because goals can be achieved once you choose to take the action required to build momentum. Once you act, you begin to move, and with movement there is friction. Friction is good because it causes energy to build. When energy builds up, it reaches a moment of monumental transformation, a point of explosive growth. With explosive growth, you are propelled through those barriers, and that is the moment in which you find your pot of gold.

When it comes to change, I believe that there are three different types of people in this world: those who make things happen, those who watch things happen, and those who wonder, "What in the world just happened?" It's a principle I learned in my years as a Mary Kay Sales Director. What category are you in now? Is it really where you want to be? If not, *move*! Dream your dream, set your vision, and place your vivacious goals into explosive action so that you can live the life that you were meant to live.

One biblical principle that I refer to and have posted in my office is, "Brothers, I do not consider myself yet to have taken hold of it. But one thing I do: Forgetting what is behind and straining toward what is ahead, press on toward the goal to win the prize for which God has called me heavenward in Christ Jesus" (Philippians 3:13–14). Amen, amen, indeed, indeed!

CHAPTER 2

Childhood: My Parents'

C hildhood is an influential phase in each of our lives. I have to say that my childhood was filled with precious memories of unconditional love. I had two amazingly loving parents who met at the ripe young age of fourteen.

Their story begins with their meeting in the Common Learning class at Thurston High School in Redford, Michigan, in the tenth grade. My dad was the oldest child of three children, and my mother was the oldest of eight.

I will first start with my dad, Richard Stuart Turner Sr. My grandmother and namesake, Elaine, was his mother, and she met my grandfather, whom I never knew, when she was twenty-one years old. They met at an Arthur Murray dance class, where she was a dance teacher. She was wooed by his handsome stature, and his charismatic aura drew her into his world. Little did she know that, not only would she end up pregnant without a ring on her finger, but also, the love of her life was married to another woman, with other children. He was a gambler and a cheat, or so the story goes. Remember, this happened in the forties, a time when this type of family situation was considered scandalous. Elaine decided to keep the baby, my dad, Richard. After his birth, Elaine and Richard lived with my great-grandmother, Ida. Grandma Ida absolutely adored my father. How could anyone not? He was a beautiful, black-haired baby boy with such a handsome little face and big, curious, hazel eyes. It was believed that his father was Greek, and in looking at my father, many could not deny his Greek heritage. Elaine had come from a large family who were part French-Canadian and prided herself on being a proper young woman with class and dignity. I could be wrong, but I believe that she felt embarrassed about putting a scar or causing a ripple in the fine silk tapestry of the family legacy she wanted to create. She had the grace of a princess and looked like a goddess. She was the beauty of her family.

She went on to marry another man, whom, incidentally, she also met at Arthur Murray dance studio. His name was Matt, and he fell head over heels in love with her. He wanted to marry her and take care of her "little Ricky." They drove to Chicago, got married, and even met Liberace, the first publicized flamboyant gay entertainer. He sang for them that night, and for many years Liberace sent Elaine a little gift at Christmas. After their marriage, Matt and Elaine settled in Michigan. Matt wanted to adopt Richard, but Elaine refused his request. I am not sure if it was pride or the love she felt for the first man who stole her heart that was the catalyst for her decision, but this one decision affected my father's life. Elaine got pregnant with her second child and decided during her pregnancy that she would not be able to handle having an infant and a toddler, so she sent Richard to live with great-grandmother Ida and my great-grandfather Russ. Elaine saw my father only every Sunday. It should be mentioned that Richard's biological father would stop in occasionally at Ida's house to visit him and give Ida money to help support Richard, but Elaine put a stop to this because she said that it was "too confusing for the child" to have his biological father come to visit. My dad lived with his grandparents until he was nine years old and became extremely close and connected to his youngest aunt, my great-auntie Sue-Sue. She was in her teens and was dating the love of her life, my great-uncle Don, who became a big brother to my dad. He would take my dad out for ice cream, and my dad truly became the third wheel on Don and Suzanne's numerous dates. Oh, my aunt Sue-Sue was the best. She treated us all with such love, and she would host the best Christmas parties where she would give each child a special box of homemade chocolates. It was one of the highlights of my youthful memories of Christmas. When Richard was about nine years old and still living with Ida, she was diagnosed with breast cancer, and his world changed yet again. At this point, the family decided that it would be best if Richard went back to live with his mother Elaine, stepfather Matt, and baby sister, Leslie, who was six years old. Even though Elaine refused to allow my dad's stepfather, whom I call Pop-Matt, to adopt my dad, Richard decided to use Matt's surname, Preston, in school. When Richard was twelve years old, Elaine had another daughter, my aunt Lori, the baby of the family. My dad adored his baby sister. He would take her on walks in the stroller not only because he loved her but also because it was a good way to meet girls, he said. Up until the day he died, he always was her protector. As the years went by, especially during his teenage years, my dad felt unaccepted, unappreciated, undervalued, misunderstood, incomplete and honestly unloved until the day he met my mom.

Sandy, or Sandra Carol, is my mom. She was the eldest of eight children—two biological and five half-siblings, on her maternal side. Her mother and father, my grandparents, were also young when they met—too young and immature to understand and commit to a life of love. Yet they married when my grandmother was only seventeen years old. My grandfather, Edgar Shepley, was twenty-one years old when they met. He had just been discharged from the army after serving in World War II, after which he suffered from undiagnosed PTSD resulting from seeing his best friend die, which he shared with me a few years before he died. He received a Purple Heart for his service, which I still have today. He referred to me as the "rose amongst the thorns," but sometimes my male cousins refer to me as a "thorn amongst the roses" in a joking manner … I think.

At that time, Edgar's sister, my great-aunt Dolores, a.k.a. Dody, worked with my grandmother at the five-and-dime store, Kresge's. They, my maternal grandparents, met through Dody in December and got married in March. They had my mother, Sandy, on October 6, 1946. They were so young and still developing as people, yet now they had another person, Sandy, to love and care for. Due to their youth and immaturity, Sandy was bounced around from different family members throughout her young life. In her second- to third-grade year, she lived at her mother's boyfriend's house in Walled Lake for two weeks, and then she was tossed around to numerous family members, including aunts, uncles, her father and his girlfriend, and her grandmother's house in just one year.

It was so crazy and overwhelming for a child her age that she does not even remember most of this time in her life because her little, tiny soul was most likely on autopilot, just trying to get through each day. She must have some amazing spirit guides and guardian angels. She lived literally out of a brown paper bag during this time and sometimes was moved in the middle of the night. During a time in her young life, she lived in Brightmoor, Detroit, with her mother and some "ladies of the night," but thankfully, through the grace of God, her uncle Gaff came in the middle of the night to rescue her.

From the age of seven to nine, Sandy lived with her paternal grandmother, Marguerite Shepley, but not her grandfather, Edgar Shepley Sr., because at that time he was living somewhere else (yet another story). She loved that time with my great-grandmother, her mother, and her uncles, aunts, and cousins. Marguerite was a loving, caring German woman, yet she could put my great-grandfather and the kids into their places when needed.

One of my favorite visions of this sweet, loving household is from my mom's description of the bus driver's face when she would come to pick up the kids for school. Out would march numerous boys and girls with lunch pails from this thousand-square-foot bungalow to board the school bus. The bus driver must have wondered where in the world these kids slept in that house.

A young couple in the neighborhood found favor with my mom, invited her for dinner, and exposed her to the arts by taking her to plays. It is a memory that my mom still holds onto. When Sandy was in her high school years, she was called to the office one day to speak to someone at one of the social workers' offices, who ended up being the young married man from her youth. He told her that he just wanted to see how she was doing. He and his wife had lost contact with Sandy after the age of nine, when my grandmother took her out of the state for a few years. His concern for her well-being touched my mother's heart.

Another favorite, yet playfully disturbing, vision I have is when my mom, while visiting her aunt Parker in Flint, Michigan, on some weekends, would witness her older male cousins use their BB guns and shoot at their younger male cousins as they ran through the open fields behind Aunt Parker's house. My mom and her other female family members were inside cleaning and doing dishes, while her male cousins were causing mischief and mayhem in the fields. I will assure you that they all survived, and therefore there is no need to call Child Protective Services. Maybe that harsh, abrupt, yet loving environment equipped them for their own calling.

When my mom was nine years old, my grandmother Helen moved herself and my mother to Galax, Virginia. Despite the poverty environment and living with her maternal grandparents along with her mother, who eventually left her behind, Sandy describes those years as some of her most cherished childhood memories. She had the least yet also had the most, which for her was years filled with love and happiness. After about three years there on the family farm, Helen left my mom there and decided to join the carnival to experience the circus life. She ended up settling in Houston, Texas, without any of her three children—Sandy, Uncle Jim (a.k.a. Shep), or Uncle Rick. Her grandmother, Hesse Bell Frost (née Absher), was born through her maternal bloodline of McCoy lineage, and I have a photo of her Galax family, which I keep with the cherished McCoy tea kettle. I will pass along the photo and the tea kettle to my own children.

While living in Galax, my mom wore hand-me-down clothes and shoes. When she needed a dress, my great-grandmother, to whom I referred as Grandmother Frosting, would make her dresses out of the cattle's feed bag material. My mother described the fabric as a beautifully printed material, which Grandmother Frosting sewed into a dress on her treadle sewing machine. My mother's aunts, twins May and Gay, were just four years older than her and looked out for her. My mom is a hugger. The reason she hugs so fiercely is that she never felt that consistently genuine love from her parents. One memory my mom shared with me was a day when she was alone in the cornfield and felt a cold, dark void in her heart and soul. She cried and cried and just asked God why her parents didn't love her. That story still brings chills to my heart and soul. That beautiful brown-eyed, cherub-faced sweetheart felt so alone.

The children were on public assistance and therefore received free schoolbooks, a clothing allowance, and free lunches. Because my mother was not registered to my Grandmother Frosting's household, she did not receive any public assistance and had to leave the classroom a half hour early to clean dishes in the school kitchen to earn her free lunch. When everyone else was out on the playground, my mom was eating her lunch. This went on for a while, but then Grandmother Frosting decided to see if my mom could also receive state assistance. After filing the application for Sandy, Grandmother Frosting discovered that the state wanted to know why Sandy was not with her biological parents. After the state got involved, agents investigated my mother's identity and the reason her parents were not supporting her. This is when Virginia Social Services got involved and advised the family that if Sandy's parents did not come and retrieve her, she would become a ward of the state. After my mother's Michigan family received word of this, my grandfather Eddie and his sister, Dody, drove down to Virginia and picked up my mother. She was twelve years old when she returned to Michigan and was reunited with her family there. She lived with her biological father and stepmother, Marian, in Redford, Michigan through her graduation. She describes those years as the worst years of her youthful life. Marian was so desperately jealous of Sandy that she made her life miserable. My mom described this time of her life as a parallel of the story of Cinderella—not too warm and fuzzy.

The day my mother graduated from high school was the day she packed her bags and moved back in with her paternal grandmother, Marguerite Shepley, in Redford, Michigan. She lived there with her aunts, uncles, and paternal grandparents. She loved that time. She lived with them until she married my father on April 10, 1965.

The wonderful thing about being raised with an extended family is that you form special lifelong bonds, like those my mom created. Our family bond extends beyond our first cousins. It reaches to second cousins and some first cousins once removed. I am not sure of the correct lineage titles, but I am sure that my first cousin once removed, Michael Marihugh, also known as Turk, could clarify the exact titles that we all hold. He is the keeper of the family lineage and family tree. That is another special part of my family: we all have nicknames. God, please help the boyfriends and girlfriends who become a part of our family because they will have to learn not only our birth names but also our nicknames. My mom and her "sister-cousins," Sharon and Darlene, met every Wednesday for some girl time—another thing I love about my family.

Despite my mother's dysfunctional childhood, I have to say that her parents, my maternal grandparents, showered me with love and support throughout my youth and into my adulthood. Maybe they felt that they needed to right a wrong or maybe they just had time to mature. I absolutely loved them both with all my heart. They made me feel special and loved. My grandmother Helen sent money to my mom in my early years to help cover the expenses of my dance education, which I could have never experienced without her financial support. My grandfather would always give me a lucky two-dollar bill, many of which I still have today. I cherish them. When he would come to town, he would stop by Dunkin Donuts and buy a dozen donuts to bring to our house. He always remembered to buy me a double chocolate donut.

Being the oldest of their own families, my parents forged their own paths in life, and despite their dysfunctional upbringings, they did have wonderful relatives who looked out for them and loved them. They had a survival mentality and did not let the negative circumstances define their characters or their futures. They focused on the positive that life had to offer, and once their worlds collided, they forged their own lifelong bond and commitment to not only their marriage but also the legacy they created.

They provided me and my brother with a somewhat functional household filled with support, love, and consistency, sprinkled with some spankings, slaps, and verbal arguments. But you know what? I wouldn't have changed it one bit because it was one of those building blocks to my foundation that has brought me to the exact place that I need to be—right here in this moment.

My parents did the absolute best that they could at the time; they had my brother at nineteen years old and me at twenty-two years old. They were able to provide and create a more stable environment than they had in their own childhoods. Do not get me wrong—they were young so they made mistakes, like we all do, but through those mistakes they managed to raise two successful children and achieve fifty years of marriage.

My brother and I planned a huge fiftieth wedding anniversary party for our parents, less than a month before my father's death. My parents never had a big wedding or reception, and it was important that they celebrate their half century of marriage with an enormous celebration honoring their love and life together. The celebration was an exciting event to plan, yet in the back of my mind, it felt like my dad's living wake.

Family members took time off from work and flew into Michigan from all over the United States to be a part of this celebration. We all stayed at the Frankenmuth Bavarian Inn, which is nestled in the quaint village of Frankenmuth, Michigan—a settlement known for its Bavarian architecture, family-style chicken dinners, and the 365-day Bronner's Christmas Wonderland store. Despite the touristy feel, it is a lovely town with wonderful food and shops and a loving family atmosphere, a perfect setting for this ultimate love gathering.

We all knew that it would most likely be the last time that our extended families would be able to see my father alive. His hospice nurses, the best, provided my dad with Adderall to help boost his energy to make it through the two-day celebration.

The ceremony was magical. My parent's lifelong friend Monsignor Zenz officiated the ceremony of renewing the marital vows. Another lifelong friend and a former band member, Marc Cabrera, put together a phenomenally magical musical soundtrack of songs that my dad wrote and sang with his band, Rhapsody, back in the 1970s through early 1980s along with a photo slideshow put together by another family member, Tom

Posner. The slideshow began with my parents' childhoods and followed them like a memory capsule through the years of their marriage, the births of my brother and me, and the births and growth of their grandchildren, along with scattered memories with family, friends, and their wonderful neighbors. It was magical, to say the least.

One of the absolute best gifts that we presented at the anniversary party was the video that Marc had recorded with my dad less than two months before he died, with Marc's beautiful and talented daughter, Isabella Cabrera. If you get a chance, search YouTube for "Miracles, Rick Turner & Isabella Cabrera"[8] and feel the magic as you transcend to another dimension of true faith, love, and light. Thank you, Marc, Isabella and Tom, for allowing us to experience these treasured memories, which we will forever cherish.

As it happened, the weekend we chose to celebrate my parents' anniversary was the same weekend as the annual balloon festival in Frankenmuth. The night after the party, my dad wanted to see the balloons as they put on their light show in the field behind the hotel compound. We pushed his wheelchair outside so he could watch the balloons scattered in the field as they prepared for their takeoff the next morning. I will never forget the look of pure excitement on my dad's face as he watched them. A balloonist would release the heat in the burner to cause the balloon to float up into the dark night sky and then release the burner to cause the balloon to descend, while the light of the flames danced within the colorful tapestry of the fabric of the balloons. I can promise you that I will never look at another hot air balloon without thinking of my dad. I literally have tears in my eyes as I am typing out this memory. He truly got what life was about—love, light, and magic. He forever changed me in that moment. He was so sickly sitting in his wheelchair that weekend, but he held on because he wanted to celebrate fifty years of life with his beautiful bride, my amazing mama, Sandy.

During the anniversary party and the two days that followed, everyone got to spend a little bit of time talking with my mom and dad. The day

---

[8] "Miracles." Performed by: Rick Turner and Isabella Cabrera. Written by Isabella & Marc Cabrera & Brian Welton May 2015.

after the party, my dad was so exhausted that he remained lying in his bed, but each and every family member took the time to go to my parents' room, hop onto the bed with my dad, and share some beautiful memories sprinkled with laughter and tears and a few moments of utter silence, which I would compare to a "standing-in-the gap" kind of silence. In those calm, quiet moments, I witnessed their auras intertwine for just a few minutes, as if their souls were hugging and saying, "Au revoir." One of my dad's favorite quotes, which also describes this magical weekend, is, "It was such a beautiful thing." He was our beautiful thing.

CHAPTER 3

Childhood: Mine

On November 3, 1968, at 2:00 p.m., I decided to enter this world. I was the firstborn daughter but second and last child of Richard and Sandra Turner. I am a Scorpio, which is a fixed water sign known for our resourceful, brave, passionate, assertive, stubborn, distrusting, jealous, and secretive nature. We are great leaders, and due to our intuitive nature, we are always aware of the truth of situations. So do not ever try to lie to us because we can see right through it. We love truth and transparency in others. We despise dishonesty, love longtime friendships, and live through experiences and expressed emotions. We can keep your secrets, whatever they may be. We will take your secrets to our graves if need be. We are fierce and know the rules of the universe. We are dedicated to what we do and what we believe in. My parents were only twenty-two when they had me. My brother Ricky Junior was born two years before me and exactly twenty years after my dad was born. Their driver's license numbers are literally only one digit different. He and my father were Virgos, an Earth sign with the quality of a mutable nature. Known for their loyal, analytical, kind, hardworking, and practical nature. They love animals, books, nature, and cleanliness and despise rudeness, asking for help, and taking center stage. Nothing is left to chance with this sign because of their methodical approach to life. My mom, just like my son Grant, are Libras, an air sign and known for their cooperative, diplomatic, gracious, fair-minded, social nature. They dislike violence, injustice, loudmouths, and conformity. Libras are the peacemakers because they are drawn to balance, justice, and equality. They love partnership, and therefore it is no wonder that my parents met at the age of fourteen, married at the age of eighteen, and achieved fifty years of marriage prior to the death of my father.

I grew up in a small city surrounded by other small to medium-sized cities in the metro Detroit area. I would define our neighborhood as middle class, with post–World War II bungalows and late 1960s Michigan-style ranch homes, which is the type of house I grew up in.

My parents told me that I was an exceptionally good baby and a thumb sucker, so I learned at an incredibly young age how to soothe myself, probably because my older brother was the "Tasmanian devil." I should add here that my brother turned into an amazing brother, husband, father and man. I was extremely shy and loved playing with my dolls. I loved purple, still do, and my favorite scents are lavender and lilac, both hues of purple. My street was lined with look-alike ranch homes and black lotus trees in front of each house. In the late 1960s many young couples purchased these homes, and our street was quickly filled with young families and my many playmates. I met my childhood best friend, Tracy, at the age of two; I still have a photo of us together sitting in my blue plastic pool on my concrete driveway. I think we might have been eating popsicles, which still are one of my most favorite snacks.

At a noticeably young age, my parents let me choose my room color, and of course I chose a deep purple because I was just drawn to it. It was a nine-feet-by-ten-feet room, and after my dad applied the deep purple paint, it seemed smaller, but it was my sanctuary. I would play and dance in my room, and my young creative mind would turn it into a stage for each of my performances to my imaginary audiences.

Dance was also a huge part of my childhood and adulthood. I began dancing at the age of four. I still remember my first costume and routine. When I was five years old, I was in my first recital. I was a little skunk, and not only did I dance, but our teacher had us sing the lyrics, "Look at me. Don't you think I'm cute with my bushy tail and my furry suit? I have got style. I have got grace, and I am really high-toned. Wouldn't you like me for your very own?" The thought of it all still makes me laugh. Just to be clear, I could dance, but I definitely could *not* sing!

If you live in Michigan, you must be creative with your time during the long, cold winter months, so Tracy and I learned how to play the card game rummy. Like two little old ladies, we would play for hours and always had a ball. We would laugh so much that our tummies and cheeks would hurt. I remember one time, when we were eating chicken noodle soup, we both started laughing so hard that one of the noodles came out of Tracy's nose. Well, this got me laughing so hard that I peed my pants. You have really got to laugh at the raw and pure innocence of childhood.

Tracy and I both loved dolls, and our parents bought us each a Crissy doll during the doll craze in the early 1970s. Chrissy was a beautiful, ginger-haired, brown-eyed, cherub-faced, lifelike, eighteen-inch doll. We played with those dolls every day. Tracy's mom had five children, of which Tracy was the second, so with each addition to her family, we inherited more baby clothes for our Crissy dolls. Crissy was a special doll not only because she was lifelike but also because she had a special feature that let us adjust the length of her hair. Well, Tracy and I did not like that silly, odd-looking, long ponytails on the tops of our dolls' heads when the rest of their hair was short, so one day we cut them off. So our dolls had an odd-looking ginger stump of thick hair on the top of their heads. I think we played with our dolls until we nearly reached junior high.

In the summers, we would spend our time making sheet tents in the backyard, playing on the swing sets and in the wooden dollhouse, walking up to K-mart to get a Coke slushy and some Maybelline roll-on lip gloss, and walking down the street to Villa Bakery to buy a pizza bread, Coke, and chocolate-glazed brownie. We had lots of sleepovers and sometimes would eat dinner twice in one night, once at my house and then at her house. Boy, those were the days. It all came to an end just before we started junior high when Tracy's dad was transferred to Ohio. It broke my heart to see my best friend move. I missed her immensely.

I cried for days, weeks, and months. But I made new friends, and so did she. We saw each other a few times after her move, but then we moved on. Times were different then with no cell phones and no internet, Skype, Facebook, Instagram, or Snapchat. We are now friends on Facebook, and I like being able to catch up with her and her family, which had been my extended family for so many years.

Many times throughout life, fate takes people away and brings people together. In the sixth grade, right before Tracy left Michigan, I was assigned to Mr. Beardsley's class. He was a tall, stern man with a military background. He had a bent pinky finger, most likely an injury from the war, that made him look a little bit like a pirate. To be honest with you, in the beginning of that school year, I truly feared this man. This was the year that I became incredibly good friends with two of my "lifer girlfriends," my soul sisters Lisa and Yvonne. Yvonne lived on the same block as me, and Lisa lived one block north of us. In elementary school, we were on the cheerleading team and student council together. Little did we know that we were putting in place the foundational blocks of our lifelong friendship. "Oou-ungowa Spartan Power, one a power, two a power, give me some of that Spartan power!" I'm not sure if I spelled that cheer right or what the hell it actually meant, but I can assure you that my beautiful, full-of-love, lifelong friend Yvonne is laughing hysterically as she is reading this. I remember that Mr. Beardsley's bark was way worse than his bite, but I hated it when I would get back one of my homework assignments or papers with his big red X on it, which meant that it needed to be redone. Lisa, Yvonne, and I were in the same sixth-grade class, and Mr. Beardsley named us his Three Musketeers. We still use his title to describe our friendship today.

Throughout our years of school, we had different hobbies and interests, but despite the different friend groups we created, we maintained our special bond. As the years passed, our careers and marriages took us to different cities and states, but our uniquely intimate and honest circle of friendship has sustained us on the roller-coaster ride of life. I love the raw honesty of our friendship. We cannot pretend with one another because we have been through too much life together. That is the specialness of our friendship; we can be open, honest, and true with one another without the fear of judgment, ridicule, or rejection. I find that there is a certain kind of peace in knowing that. It is like putting on a warm blanket and fuzzy slippers on a cold day or eating your grandmother's chicken-noodle soup when you are sick with the flu. I am forever grateful for their unwavering friendship, love, support, and the joy they bring into my life.

When I was in the sixth grade, my mom decided that I was good enough to join a competitive dance studio, so she drove me to my first dance audition at a studio that was known for its winning performances and artistic, creative choreography, Masters of Dance Arts in Canton, Michigan. I was accepted to the junior competitive team and was so thrilled for the opportunity. My first friend at dance was Tammy. You know those people who have an actual sparkle in their eyes? Well, that's Tammy. Her smile was so big that it seeped into her eyes and made them sparkle. She was shorter than me, with dark wavy hair and cute little feet, and she could fill a bathing suit top like nobody's business. I, on the other hand, did not even need to wear a bra. I was long and lanky, and the only curve on my body was my round German butt. She lived in a city south of mine with a more country-like, rural feel. In the summer, I spent numerous long weekends at her house with her and her older sister, Tori, who was so fun and full of sass, which I loved. Tammy's mom, Sharon, also a fiery spirit, was my second dance mom, and Tammy's dad, Bill, was the consistent calm among the three women. Her family was a camping family, unlike mine. The one memory of my family camping was an absolutely shit-show nightmare involving my dad pitching the tent in the valley of the campground and an insane thunderstorm coming through, which led to the tent flooding. We ended up in a neighbor's pop-up trailer with fifteen of our other neighbors. The memory of this event reminds me of that part in the movie *The Perfect Storm* when the characters were pretty sure that they weren't going to make it out alive. Despite the PTSD associated with that childhood memory, camping with Tammy's family was a comforting, peaceful alternative to the childhood trauma I experienced. With Tammy's family, we had blue skies and sunshine. Tammy and I listened to her parents' eight-track cassettes in the camper and choreographed dance routines to the music. We created one routine that stands out, to "On Broadway" sung by George Benson. We went down a dirt road to perform our routine for those bystanders who watched from the RVs and tents, most likely wondering, *What in the hell are these two girls doing?* These are great memories with my sweet friend Tammy and her beautiful family.

Due to decreasing public-school enrollment during this same time frame, the city I lived in began downsizing and merging schools. I attended three different schools from seventh to ninth grade. Prior to this merger, students were considered either westsiders or eastsiders. I was an eastsider, but I really liked the fact that the downsizing of schools provided me the opportunity to meet kids from the west side of the city.

I liked my junior high and high school experiences. From sixth through the summer going into my eleventh grade, Tammy's mom and my mom drove us from city to city and state to state for local and national dance competitions. I've danced on top of the Empire State Building, in Central Park, at the Radio City Music Hall, and for the USO, but two of my favorite dance memories are the times I danced with Bob Fosse in Chicago and Gregory Hines in New York City. I loved the magnetic, magical energy of both Chicago and New York; both were so full of life. I was able to take some dance workshops with these iconic legends. I remember being called on stage with Bob Fosse! I thought, *What? Are you kidding me?* My mom was so proud and excited. Of course, this happened before cell phones, Facebook, and YouTube so there is no video evidence that I know of, but I can assure you that it did happen. The thrilling memory of this event will forever fill my heart and soul with the feeling of finally being good enough.

In my junior year, I decided that I wanted to get more involved in my high school, so I tried out for the pompon team. Due to the financial obligations of this sport, I had to choose between dance and pom. I chose pom. It was a tough decision, which at times I regret. We did not have an actual pom coach, but we all had self-discipline and practiced every day after school. Another former dancer, Melissa, and I were voted as the captain and co-captain, respectively.

Dance taught me the balance between winning and losing. In the loss, I learned to work harder because, in dancing, not everyone got a trophy or a ribbon. If you didn't place in the top three, then you didn't get anything except the burning desire in the pit of your stomach to work hard and be better, which was the drive and conviction required to win at the next year's dance competitions. Dance taught me to love myself, and at the time, with my quirky growing body, my soul needed that positive affirmation. Dance taught me the discipline and patience that my young developing soul needed, as well as how to create and think out of the box, while giving me the confidence to develop and embrace my own personal style. Dance will forever be a part of who I was, what I am, and where I am going.

I was grateful that my mom shared in my passion for dance. She and my father made many sacrifices so we could afford the expenses of my dance training and competitive dance travel. As I grew up, I was grateful that my mom was able to travel with me to my various competitions and workshops in New York City and Chicago. This time together helped solidify the strong bond I have with her today. My regret was that I should have taken more time to spend with my father to learn about his own passions. He loved his music. As I previously mentioned, he was a self-taught musician, singer, and songwriter. He was an incredibly talented man, and because he started his family at the young age of eighteen, I feel that he cut his potential musical career short. He had to get a "real" job to provide for immediate financial needs and a stable monthly income for our family. He did have a band. The guys would get together at night and have their jam sessions in our basement. I remember that the music was so loud that not only our house vibrated, but I am sure our entire street vibrated from the sound. The band members were a little younger than my dad, but they all had that late 70s, early 80s look, with long hair and bell-bottom pants. My parents were hippies and very cool hippies at that, evidenced by the glass-mirrored walls in our living room and the wooden beads that hung from the orange kitchen entryway. I really wish I would have taken the time to learn more about music from my dad, but I did not. Once, he was working with me on my vocals, and after about two painful hours, he told me, "It's OK, babe. Just stick to dancing." It is true that I am clearly not a singer, but I loved hearing him sing. His other passion was cars. Of course, this passion may have been a form of survival because we lived paycheck to paycheck, and therefore he had to learn how to fix the cars to keep them running. His first new car was a 1967 GTO. I remember this car because we sold it shortly after his death. It was a brilliant blue with black-leather interior. When I sat in the backseat, I would tell him, "Go faster, Daddy. Go faster!" This would totally stress my mom out, but my dad would go a bit faster because I absolutely loved it.

I met a lot of great peers in my childhood and teens and had some amazing teachers and administrators. The few great memories that stand out the most as I reflect on my high school years are winning the pompon state championship in 1985, seeing Yvonne be crowned homecoming queen, seeing Lisa be crowned prom queen, and cramming the entire pompon team into Candace's Oldsmobile Cutlass sedan to go to the drive-in movie theater to watch *Purple Rain*.

If I had to describe my childhood using only one word to express what I felt, it would be *loved*. I was loved. I had caring, loving, supportive parents and family, and I had some pretty kick-ass friends, who are still a huge part of my life. I have been blessed with many great soul sisters from my early toddler years of sitting in my plastic pool with my friend Tracy through throwing our caps into the air with Lisa and Yvonne on our graduation day and onto Marie, Jennifer, Marlene, and Nicole. I will introduce Marlene, the powerhouse, to you later.

Despite these awesome memories, I sometimes felt that I was not good enough or smart enough. My family's words that have rung in my ears since I was a very little girl are "She's not as smart as Ricky," "She has to work harder," and "Her looks and personality will get her through life." I know that these statements were not made with ill will or cruelty, but they stuck with me through life. My high school grades were good, and I was smart enough to get into college and complete my bachelor's degree, but I totally bombed my ACT, most likely due to my low self-confidence. My brother dropped out of college just as I was entering my senior year of high school. Due to his decision, my parents decided that they were not going to help me with my college expenses. Between my low ACT score and the fact that I would be footing the bill, I chose to attend a junior college for two years and then transfer to a university to complete my bachelor's degree, which is exactly what I did. I worked my butt off, going to college and working a nearly full-time job so I could pay for my college expenses, and I would not ever change that path. It taught me perseverance, an amazing work ethic, and time management, and I learned on that journey that I was in fact smart enough. It took me four and a half years to complete my BBA. I did not have the time or the money to be in a sorority. I didn't have a lot of friends in college because I was way too busy commuting to the university, driving to work, and returning home, where I would collapse on my bed surrounded by my notebooks, highlighters, and three-inch-thick textbooks. I never did the cap-and-gown thing because that did not really matter to me. I achieved this goal for me and only for me. I ended up moving from an office administration position into a judicial aide position with one of the local courts. And so, the transformation from childhood to adulthood began.

Recently, my mom admitted to me that when my brother and I were younger, she craved a perfect *Leave It to Beaver* type of family, lifestyle, and image. She wanted my dad, brother, and me to be perfect. Because I was a people pleaser, I quickly fell into the role of the "perfect daughter" when I was younger. I still struggle with that, and over the past three years, I've realized how it has negatively affected others and put a strain on many of my relationships. This trait, as with many traits, can initiate from ancestral karma, which we unconsciously carry into our current lifetimes. It's a part of our shadow-work that we can choose to clear. The first step is awareness, and the second is acceptance. The third step can take the longest because it requires mindfulness. You have to be completely present in each "now" moment and see yourself. Sometimes you can see yourself through your thoughts, words, and actions. Other times, you can see yourself through others. When the acceptance is complete—a.k.a. taking ownership and responsibility—you can choose to clear the ancestral flaw. The final step is forgiveness for yourself and your ancestors. There's no such thing as perfection, unless you can accept the way things are as perfectly imperfect and settle in contentment with that honesty.

I shed sweat, and tears—literal tears—over the past fifty years of my life trying to prove to this sometimes cynical, cruel, bitter world that I was good enough. After I reached my fiftieth birthday, I realized that I *was* good enough, not by the standards of others but through my higher self and through the eyes of our creator, who I refer to as God.

CHAPTER 4

Childhood: The Firstborn, Natalie and Jack

The oldest or only child bear many blessings and significant burdens. If you are one, you not only pave the way, from actual childbirth, for your younger siblings, but you also bear the brunt of the mistakes that parents make with their firstborn children. If you are the firstborn, you are the guinea pig for first-time parents. You may have had overbearing, helicopter parents because, let's face it, you were the most important thing that your parents ever created. You were their everything, and therefore they watched your every move and tried to protect you. But maybe your parents raised you with a hands-off approach, trying to give you as much freedom as possible to discover your true inner self. Regardless of the approach that your parents took, your personality and characteristic traits were developed in these younger years.

Firstborn children are natural-born leaders. They sometimes take the role of guardian and protector of their younger siblings. Firstborn children can be nurturing caregivers, or they may take on the role of the assertive, strong-willed leader.

As I shared with you, I immediately thought of my two firstborn children. My family is a blended family, and therefore I have two children who are the first and the oldest. I will first share my experiences with my oldest biological child, Natalie. Our firstborn female took the role of the nurturing caregiver, and Jack, my firstborn stepson, took the role of the dominant firstborn male. Some of the firstborn characteristics include reliability, conscientiousness, structure, caution, and control with an accelerated drive to achieve all their God-given gifts and destiny.

Since Natalie was the oldest, I raised Natalie with 100 percent of my focus, providing her every opportunity to excel in life. I surrounded her with love, support, and encouragement with the hopes that my efforts would provide her with a solid foundation for her to grow into the best that she could be in all aspects of life. I expected her to sit up, crawl, walk, and talk before the *What to Expect in the First Year* book told me she would. And of course, she did not disappoint. She was three years old when I had my second child, Grant. I remember the day she walked into the hospital room to meet her little, round-faced, black-haired, hazel-eyed brother. She ran into the hospital room with a huge smile on her face and a spark of excitement in her big, round, blue-green eyes. You know those eyes that you see in the Margaret Keane paintings? Those are the eyes that my Natalie has. Her eyes still transition from a vibrant sky blue to a Caribbean green based on her mood. After running into the hospital room, she jumped on my bed and wanted to immediately hold her baby brother and take care of him. When we got home from the hospital, she was Mommy's best helper. As soon as her baby brother cried, she would run to get him a diaper, baby powder, his binky, his blanket, or whatever she thought might soothe him. She still has the same natural nurturing instincts. When she was five, which is when experts believe that a child's personality is formed, her next sibling arrived, her baby sister Ava. She had prayed for a baby sister. With that birth, in her little five-year-old eyes, her world was complete, with a baby brother and sister to love, hold, kiss, nurture, play with, read to, and teach. She is still their mini mommy.

By the age of five, she was the entertainment for all our family gatherings. We bought her a mini stage with a curtain and microphone. Given the fact that she began dancing at the age of three, she had numerous costumes for her performances. At one family event, she told everyone that she was going to give us a show. This was during the time that Britney Spears was the new young star emerging from her years of being a Mickey Mouse Club member and actress into America's Top 40 hit list. Natalie got out her stage and her mini cassette player with attached microphone as we all waited to see what the evening performance would be. She hit the play button, opened the stage curtains with the microphone in hand and wearing her sparkling lime green costume with hot pink trim, and began singing, "Oh baby, baby." It was a riot. But she could actually sing and dance; she was a natural entertainer. Her performance was very lively. Of course, I thought Pop-Matt, her great-grandfather, was going to fall out of his chair.

She was only in sixth grade when I went back to work on a part-time basis. She was responsible for helping take care of her younger siblings with after-school snacks and getting started on their homework. She was such a huge help to me. In the summer she would help them complete their two pages of summer workbook activities, and they would all write a page in their summer journals. During those summer days, Natalie would get them lunch and monitor things until I got home. Sometimes—no, a lot of the time—I find myself still feeling guilty about all the responsibilities she had at such a young age. I worry that I expected too much from her and that maybe I took away some of her own childhood. Yet she never really complained. It seemed to be so easy for her, and I feel like the maternal part of her being loved playing mommy during that time. It was easy to forget that she was only a child herself.

When she was in eighth grade, her father and I got divorced. This was a tough year for all my children, but especially Natalie. She was so very brave and told me that she understood why we had to divorce, but let's face it, she was still a little girl and suffered the emotional effects from the fallout of divorce. I had to go back to work full-time and, once again, she stepped into the role of mini-me and was the parent to Grant and Ava when I could not be there. I was so very blessed that my firstborn was such a loving and nurturing soul. It's no wonder that she chose a career in nursing, where she continues to shine her love, light, and nurturing soul on her patients and coworkers.

Natalie is an incredibly good soul. She looks for the good in everyone, which I envy. She dreams and dreams *big*, and she achieved her goal of becoming a nurse. She has a fearless heart. When she was little, around age four, one of our neighbors would put up a huge nativity scene under an enormous pine tree in their front yard during the Christmas holiday, and each and every time we would drive home from picking her up from school, she would make me stop and roll down the window, despite the bitter cold of Michigan winters. She would sing a song that she and my dad sometimes sung together: "Jesus was a good boy, yes he is. Jesus was a good boy, yes indeed." Then one day she told me, "Mommy, I think I want to be a nun, but I have a burning desire to have children, so I think I will be a nurse instead so I can help people." I was awestruck! How could this little person whom I helped create say such a provocative statement? I laughed and told her that she could be anything or anyone she wanted to be. Before my very eyes, my gosh, that girl did it. She worked hard—and I mean *hard*—to achieve her goal. I could not be prouder of the woman she has become, earning her BSN and making an impact on so many. She believed that she could, so she did. She is fierce and awesome, yet she maintains her "Pooh-bear" heart. She still loves to watch Disney movies. I know that her own version of her knight in shining armor will arrive to sweep her off her feet and capture her heart.

My second husband, Matt, got divorced when his oldest, Jackson, was only in the first grade. Jackson was the kingpin of his younger siblings. After the divorce, he found himself in the role of the dominant male of his mother's household at the mere age of six. He had to become tough, mentally and physically. He is hardwired and hard driven. He was tough on his younger siblings, Marco and Ana. I cannot tell you too many stories about Jack in his early childhood because I did not know him then. He was in the fourth grade when I met Matt. He got to sit in the front seat with his dad and always got an extra scoop of ice cream and extra Coke just because he was the oldest.

When we married, Natalie was in the tenth grade and Jackson was in the fifth grade. Jackson went from being the firstborn to somewhere in the middle of our blended family: Natalie, Grant, Ava, Jackson, Marco, and Ana. This was a difficult transition for all of them, but I feel it was extremely difficult for Jackson, especially because he inherited an older brother. Still, Natalie was ultimately the oldest and therefore was expected to behave and react in a manner that her younger five siblings would model. Oh, the pressure that she endured! Yet I believe in my heart that the experience molded her into the badass woman she is today, and for that reason alone, I have no regrets.

Jackson struggled for many years to figure out his new role in our blended family. I would be lying to you if I told you it was easy because it was not—for him, for his father, or for me—yet we got through it all. He is doing fantastic, and we are so heartfully proud of the man that he has become. I hope and pray that, as he continues to mature and eventually begins his own family, he will realize the positive impact that our love and discipline have added to his positive characteristics.

Firstborn or only children can exhibit the traits of leadership, cooperative nature, organization, self-driven, goal setters, achievers, and scholars, but they also have the pitfalls of being overbearing, insensitive, self-critical, worriers, anxious, aggression, stressed, minimalist thinking, narcissistic, and being too serious.

I feel that our firstborns bear the more positive attributes and I hope that they know the love and gratitude we hold in our hearts for the roles that they play.

CHAPTER 5

Childhood: In the Middle, Grant and Marco

People who were middle children while growing up have to accept that another human being came not only before them but also after them. Many middle children end up being content with *not* being the object of attention. They come to the realization at a noticeably young age that they will never receive the same attention that their older or younger siblings received yet seem to handle this with grace and understanding. What is grace? Grace is the ability to understand and comprehend others' feelings with sympathy, tolerance and forgiveness. Please note that their understanding does not mean that they were not hurt by feeling ignored or left out, nor does it mean that it is an acceptable way to parent. Honestly, as a parent of three biological children and three stepchildren, the idea of middle-child syndrome breaks my heart. After the blending of our families we ended up with *two* middle children: Grant, my biological middle son, and Marco, my middle son from my second marriage. Interestingly, these two children bear many similarities and hold a huge place inside my heart.

Without reading anything from professionals about what the middle child embodies, I can tell you from my own experiences that middle children rock. They are self-resilient, pliable, mutable, flexible, elastic, resilient, and supple. They are sweet, kind, loving, sympathetic, enduring, reliable, strong, creative, ingenious, innovative, adventurous, and original, and God, do I love these qualities about them.

Despite the fact that, per the professionals, second-born or middle children rely on the firstborn as their role models, they usually shoot off into a different direction in order to find their own place not only in the family unit but in the world and universe. Sometimes, if the second-born is the same sex as the first, they can take over the firstborn child's role, prestige, and status in the family unit.

I will share an example of what these middle children are like. Believe it or not, in this very moment as I am writing about middle children, my son Marco injured himself. I took a brief break from writing because I might have the smallest bladder in the universe of all bladders. In the bathroom, I discovered a bloody crime scene. There was blood all over the place. Trying not to completely freak out, I decided to follow the trail of blood, which led to Marco's room and then continued to the upstairs bathroom, where I found my husband and Marco. Marco had his leg hanging over the sink with a huge, two-inch cut near his peroneal tendon, bleeding profusely. I said, "What happened?" Marco said that, while getting out of the shower, he hit his foot on the shower door and cut himself. I had to laugh out loud because, of course, being a middle child, he didn't want to make a big scene about his injury, so he just discreetly walked up the stairs, trailing blood, to take care of it himself. We cleaned off his wound, put ice on it to stop the bleeding, and bandaged him up. This is what I absolutely love, love, love about middle children. They never make a big deal over big deals in life.

My biological son, Grant, bears many of the middle-child characteristics. One specific memory I have of Grant was when I threw this enormous third Thomas the Tank Engine birthday party for him. We involved all our family, friends, and neighbors. Grant was a Thomas junkie. He watched every DVD ever made about Thomas the Tank Engine, Sir Topham Hatt, Percy the Small Engine, Gordon the Big Express Engine, Henry the Green Engine, James the Red Engine, Edward the Blue Engine, Toby the Tram Engine, Emily the Steam Engine—I could go on, but I will spare you. Because I am a go-big-or-go-home kind of person, I rented a real Thomas the Tank Engine to come to the house and surprise Grant. I remember it so clearly: as I heard "Dan, Dan the Choo-Choo Man" pulling up in front of our house with his train and passenger cars, I looked at Grant and said, "Your train has arrived." Grant looked up at me with his big hazel eyes, grabbed my hand for security, and walked cautiously next to my side into the front yard. The other kids ran around us screaming with excitement and jumped into the seats in the passenger car. Grant, on the other hand, wanted absolutely no part of it. The conductor gave him his own special conductor hat and a wooden block whistle that sounded like a train when he blew into it. Grant took the items, began to cry, and ran into his room. The driver took off without Grant, yet his two sisters, cousins, and friends were on the choo-choo train. As I waved goodbye to the kids, my brother asked," Is there any other adult on that train?" *No*, I thought, *we just let a stranger take our most prized possession, our children, without any other adult and without a second thought.* No worries—Dan the Choo-Choo Man brought them all back safe and sound after the six-block ride around the neighborhood. Grant eventually went on the train, but it took some coaxing on my part. When we sang him happy birthday, he just stared down at his Thomas cake, then covered his face with his hands, and cried. He was such a shy baby boy. Unlike his older sister who loved a captive audience, Grant wanted nothing to do with it. He learned how to handle his shyness and would quietly escape the large family gatherings to play in his room with his favorite cousin, Nick. When he was placed in uncomfortable settings or situations, such as large crowds, groups of people, and classrooms, he learned how to tap into his humor, which eased his anxiety and shyness. Several times throughout Grant's school years, his teachers would send me e-mails saying, "Grant just made me laugh in class today. No one else got the joke because he thinks at such a high level and his humor can only be appreciated by someone who's older." This is how he learned to cope in life. He is blessed with some lifelong friends. These boys were introduced to one another at a remarkably young age, while in their car seats and strollers at our Rosedale Gardens neighborhood play group. They are healthy, handsome, brilliant, talented young men who have achieved great successes in their own lives while maintaining their childhood friendships: Grant, Peter, Bennett, and Neil. I love our Rosedale Garden's "Brat Pack."

Middle children can exhibit inconsistency. They can be quiet and shy, yet sociable and outgoing, impatient or laid back, competitive or not competitive, rebellious or peacemaking. Studies reveal that "middles" are more grounded than the first- and last-born children later in life, yet some struggle with their underlying resentment and anger. For those who are dealing with such anger, you need to figure out how to communicate your emotions in a positive, constructive manner so you can release the anger and resentment and live a life filled with love and light.

CHAPTER 6

Childhood: The Baby, Ava and Ana

"Last but never least" is the true belief and motto of the baby of the family. My youngest biological daughter, Ava, is a great example of this motto. She was five years younger than her sister and eighteen months younger than her brother, yet she never allowed that difference to stop her from being first. I hope my older two kids laugh when I share some of these stories with you because I know it will seem to them like it happened yesterday.

Ava had to be held by me all the time. I mean, literally, I had to put her in one of those front carriers so I could do my other motherly and wifely duties without her screaming her head off and turning a lovely shade of crimson red. When she was about nine months old, she had her first seizure—scared the hell out of me. I sat her down on the floor next to Grant so I could run upstairs to get something. I was not even upstairs for thirty seconds and suddenly, I heard a *thump*. I ran downstairs to find her lying on her back, turning blue, and obviously not breathing. I grabbed her and flipped her over, pounding on her back while asking Grant if she had put anything into her mouth. Of course, he was only two and a half, so obviously the conversation was limited. I yelled to their father to call 9-1-1. As he was speaking to the dispatcher, Ava became lifeless in my arms. I thought she had died, but then she started to take in little, short, shallow breaths. The firefighters arrived, and after examining Ava, they told me that she had suffered a seizure. There was no family history of seizures, and I was extremely uneducated about them, yet overly concerned. She was exhausted that night and into the next day. I realized that when she got upset, she would cry so hard that she would stop breathing, one of our primal survival instincts.

She loved only two adults in her life at the time: me and my father, Papa Rick. Do not get me wrong—she would tolerate her biological father when I or my father were not there, but if someone else tried to hold her or if she got mad or hurt, she would cry. I realized that if I could get to her fast enough after she began to cry, I could get her to take a breath by either splashing a little water or blowing hard into her face, and she would be OK. Sometimes that would not happen. On one specific date that I will never forget, we were having a Father's Day celebration at my parents' house. I was inside helping my mom, and through their family room window I saw Ava fall on the cement driveway. It was not a bad fall, but it was bad enough that she began to cry. I immediately knew that if I did not get to her in time, it would end with a seizure. I did not make it to her in time, and this time it was a bad seizure—so bad that she was not regaining consciousness. Firefighters arrived and took us to the hospital, but the doctors at the local hospital were so concerned about her that they transported us to a larger hospital with a specialized pediatric unit. I remember the medical staff buzzing in and out of the room as Ava laid on the bed with a postictal stare off to the right. This altered state of consciousness of a patient who just had a seizure should last only from five to thirty minutes, but due to the severity of her seizure, it lasted many hours with Ava. I stood on one side of the bed and her father on the other. I remember just praying, praying so hard, *God, please make her OK. Please bring her back to us.* The doctors were not sure what the effects of the seizure would be or when she would return to a conscious state. After hours, which felt like lifetimes, she woke, just like that. She looked from side to side and said, "Mommy, Daddy." Tears of joy streamed down my face as I took her into my arms and planted butterfly kisses all over her cherub face. She had numerous tests run, including an MRI and CT scans to confirm that there were no lesions or tumors. The doctors told me that Ava was just stubborn and held her breath when she was upset. I honestly did not believe that a baby or toddler would consciously hold her breath when she was upset, hurt, or did not get her way. I do believe in the possibility that babies and toddlers, when crying, may create a blockage in the airflow because of the development of the esophagus. When our bodies do not get enough oxygen, it can lead to a seizure. The medical team advised us that she would eventually grow out of them.

Once we got Ava home from the hospital, we explained to her older siblings that we had to be careful with her because we were trying to limit the number of seizures she had and eventually eliminate them. Natalie and Grant had witnessed her seizure and were fearful of having their baby sister go through that again, so whatever Ava wanted, they gave her—the last cookie, the last sucker, Grant's binky, and so on. Eventually she did grow out of them, but by this time she was used to getting whatever she wanted.

I have always said, "I'm a Jag woman in a minivan world." When the kids were younger, I had a booster seat and two car seats at one time. When she was able to walk, Ava made sure she pushed her way to the front of the sliding van door so she could be first in her seat. Guess what happened when I arrived at the destination? Yes, Ava would jump out of her car seat so fast and push past her two older siblings to make certain that she was the first one out of the van. She was insanely competitive and always had to win. She was a fierce player of mancala and would play and beat anyone who was willing to sit down and play with her. Ava has grown into a beautiful soul. She is loving, caring, understanding and exhibits immense empathy for every person who crosses her path. One of the most rewarding complements I receive about Ava comes from her friends. They tell me that Ava is the best friend that they have and the sweetest person that they know.

When I met Matt, Ana, the baby of his family and only girl, was almost four years old. She was fiercely independent, tough, always on the go, and very social. She never really seemed to have that sense of fear of strangers and absolutely loved being the center of attention. Because she was the only girl, she pretty much got whatever she wanted. When Matt and I married, Ana was still the baby of our blended family, but she had to share her tiara with two older sisters. Natalie was incredibly good with Ana and loved watching Disney movies with her. Ava and Ana shared a room. Ava was a little bit jealous of her new younger sister because not only did she have to share my attention with another child, but this child was now the baby of the family, and she was a girl too. Ava moved from being the baby to somewhere in the middle. Ana, like Ava, is competitive and hates to lose at anything. But unlike Ava, Ana has more of the dramatic flair, like Natalie—you know, the eye-rolling, stomping off, and slamming the door kind of dramatic flair. She is the baby but looks and acts much older than she truly is because she has two older sisters to model and copy. Both Ava and Ana are loving and compassionate. They share similar and yet different personality traits of being the babies of our families.

Youngest children usually display traits of being charismatic, affectionate, people-oriented, persistent, relaxed, transparent, and entertaining, but they also have the pitfalls of being or appearing manipulative, undisciplined, too assertive, gullible, indecisive, absent-minded, and self-centered.

You can spend so much of your time and energy placing blame on your parents for the mistakes they made or on your birth order, but the harsh reality of life is that, ultimately, you need to take ownership of the choices you have made and start taking control of your life. How do you do this? Well, you first start with learning about who you really are, and once you figure that out, the next questions will be who you want to be and what your life goals and purposes are.

CHAPTER 7

The Brink of Adulthood:
The Late Teens and Early Twenties

This might be a harsh reality for late teenagers and twenty-somethings, but your age does not guarantee your arrival to adulthood. As the famous quote from Ralph Waldo Emerson states, "Life is a journey, not a destination."[9]

One of the misconceptions of life is that, when we hit important mile-markers in life—like when we're five we go to kindergarten, when we're sixteen we get a driver's license, when we're eighteen we get to vote, when we're twenty-one we get to drink—all the needed knowledge and required wisdom will magically appear. The real question is whether or not you are ready for responsibilities of the freedom.

Life is most definitely a journey, shaded with colors that blend from one event into another, leaving a beautiful canvas of intermingling life events and lessons. The gradual transitions of life help soften the lines and fill in the gaps between infancy to toddlerhood and on through adulthood. I just love this, and I think it is super cool. It is the ebb and flow of energy, our energy.

---

[9] [RWEJ] 1845 [Copyright 1844], Essays: Second Series by Ralph Waldo Emerson, Second Edition, Essay: II Experience Start Page 49, Quote Page 65, James Munroe and Company, Boston.

What I loved about my late teens and twenties was freedom. I was not married, and I did not have any children, not even a dog or a cat. My only responsibility was myself. It was so freeing. I got to choose which college I wanted to attend, where I wanted to work, with whom I wanted to hang out, and what I wanted to do. The humor is that when you are at this point in your life, you really do not bask in the glory of this freedom. Rather, you crave the next chapter of your life.

My personal struggles during this time, as I touched on earlier, were my own self-confidence and, let's face it, taking the time to enjoy the freedom I had. Between working and going to college full-time, I did not have a lot of time for myself during this self-discovery phase. Maybe I did have the time, but I chose not to use it to fully embrace my freedom. It was my lack of awareness that I truly was the painter of my own canvas and the author of my own novel. I kept listening to other people who gave me timelines that I should follow for my own life. You know, when you are twenty-one, you should be graduating with your bachelor's degree. When you are twenty-three, you should be in a serious relationship. When you are twenty-five, you should be married. When you are thirty, you should have three kids.

My hopes and prayers for my own children are that they take the time to make these years adventurous. Take this time of freedom to really find out who you are, where you are in life, and what you genuinely want, while taking responsibility with these freedoms.

It takes time to figure out where you want to go and who you want to be. I pray that they take the time to try new things, eat exotic foods, travel the country, and travel the world. I pray that they do not settle into the mediocrities of life. I hope that they hold out for "the one" who turns their worlds upside down, makes their stomachs swirl with butterflies, and makes their heads spin with fairy dust. I hope that when they find that person, they are filled with such a strong magnetic field of divine energy that with each touch, their bodies and souls are filled with electric shockwaves. I pray that those shockwaves pulse through their veins, and fill their hearts, bodies, minds, and souls with more love than they ever imagined possible. I hope they find mates who love them where they are yet pushes them to be the best that they can be in each season of their lives—a soulmate who encourages personal growth and support yet gives them room to spread their wings while flying by their side. I pray that they each find a person who is spiritually-filled, loving, caring, honest, trustworthy, hard-working, fun, supportive, emotionally grounded, intelligent, loyal, open-minded, free from antisocial activities and addictions, and non-abusive. I pray that they're never afraid to ask why, to question things that no longer make sense, and to rely on their intuition and strategic thinking skills, which aid them in connecting the dots to discern the difference between what they are told and what is actually truth.

When I think of my children, all grown adults, I cannot help but smile because I know that they are mentally and physically healthy, happy individuals who are paving their own life paths as authors of their own novels. On their journeys, they will learn more about who they are and what their true life purposes are. As their mother (or "smother"), I am proud of the people they are, all uniquely different, and they fill my smiling heart with pride and joy.

CHAPTER 8

Rosedale Gardens: My Early Adulthood, Motherhood, and Midlife Blessings

I f you have ever wondered what it would be like to live in a *Leave It to Beaver* type of neighborhood in the mid 1990s throughout 2019, I can tell you. I married my first husband on September 2, 1993. We wanted to find a house close to both of our parents, who still lived in Garden City where we both grew up. We stumbled upon a quaint little neighborhood in south Livonia, with pillars at each of the Plymouth Road entrances. The streets were lined with an assortment of different mature trees that covered the front yards and English-styled blacktopped streets with their shade. This was one of the first neighborhoods developed in Livonia in the late 1920s and 1930s and had become a historic district located on eight streets and platted by the Shelden Land Company in the 1920s. The first house in Rosedale Gardens was the Harsha house, built in 1925. This neighborhood survived the Great Depression, World War II, the Korean War, the Cold War, and COVID-19. When we moved into this neighborhood, little did I know the impact it would have not only on my own life but also, on the lives of my children.

There was and still is something so magical about this neighborhood. I am not sure if I can pinpoint exactly what the magic is for you, but I feel it is a combination of many things. To start, one thing I love about this neighborhood is the differently styled houses, most of which will soon be able to claim one hundred years of existence. There have been additions and additions on those additions, which makes each house as unique as a thumbprint. The other component to the magic of the neighborhood is the people who live in these houses. This tucked-away community has a strong family feel to it. The energy there is pure love. Annually, the neighborhood hosts Christmas house tours, Santa visits, garden walks, 5K runs, Easter egg hunts, a Halloween parade, an Independence Day parade, and a picnic at the local Mies Park. It is conveniently close to shopping and entertainment and only twenty minutes from downtown Detroit. I was so very blessed to purchase my first home there. It was a 1927 brick bungalow with a fireplace, wooden floors, 1920s porcelain-tiled bathrooms and kitchen, and a little covered front porch, and it was the perfect place to start a family.

The houses in this neighborhood were loaded with charm and had their own unique character. After having my first child, I developed wonderful friendships with the other young mothers in my neighborhood. We started a moms' playgroup that met every Friday morning. We rotated houses, and no matter the weather, everyone showed up with a dish to pass and our children in tow, like little ducklings. The kids would play while the moms would share laughter and tears. So many lifelong bonds were created during that time for not only the mothers but also for the children. My middle son, Grant, is still friends with the young men that I previously referred to as the "Brat Pack" of Rosedale Gardens. They first met when they were literally in car seats shortly after their births. Our group had a maternity suitcase that we would fill with all types of seasonal and sized maternity clothes. As soon as someone became pregnant again, she got the suitcase. We also had Brenda, the saint of all motherhood saints, and she had the "magic chair." It was a baby rocker that was so fluffy with stuffing that, when any of us put our crying baby into it, they would magically fall asleep. Brenda shared this chair with all of us, and let me tell you—it worked! As the kids got older, the moms began a book club. Unfortunately, because of my part-time job at the time, I was able to meet for only a few of these monthly book studies, but I can assure you that the Boa Book Club is still operating at full force. The Arden Street neighbors began a euchre group that expanded to other streets, including mine. We get together monthly for some fun-loving euchre, good laughs, good food, and some spirits to lighten the load of our long weeks. I am so incredibly grateful for these women in my life and the positive impact that they have had on my life and my children's lives. Thank you all for your love, laughter, support, and friendship through the past twenty-five years of my life. I cannot even imagine life without any of you.

As I said, it's a magical neighborhood that I hold close to my heart for so many reasons, but in the late summer of 2019, due to the fact that my husband and I had such a large family, we sold that home and moved to another city farther west. We were so lucky to move into such a wonderful new neighborhood with fabulous new neighbors, like Kim and Scott. I refer to them as my fairy neighbors because they all have white-blonde hair and flutter around creating magnificent gardens and homemade treats. I am grateful for my new friendships and my old friendships, which have sustained the distance.

PART 2
Your Actions

Photographed by Lainie Morrison-Fryer

CHAPTER 9

Love

Love is patient, love is kind. It does not envy, it does not boast, it is not proud. It does not dishonor others, it is not self-seeking, it is not easily angered, and it keeps no record of wrongs. Love does not delight in evil but rejoices with the truth. It always protects, always trusts, always hopes, always perseveres. Love never fails. (1 Corinthians 13:4–8a)

This is one of the most well-known quotes about love. It is such a simple truth that we all know, yet each of us has failed at one point or another in love. This failure does not mean that we stop striving to achieve that level of love. As humans, we still need to strive to learn more about true, unconditional, divine love. As we work toward loving at a higher frequency, like the way God our Father loves us, we become more enlightened in the understanding of what unconditional divine love looks and feels like. This starts with self-love.

The reason I feel that this type of unconditional divine love can be challenging at times is because, number one, we are human. We cannot possibly love to the level of God and his Son, Jesus, in this 3D world, but we need to have a mark to strive for, a goal to hit. It raises the bar of excellence for us and gives us a target that we can aim for in our daily lives. One of the most profound quotes about the silent killer of marriages is by Derek Harvey. He wrote, "The reason marriages end in divorce is because of one thing … unmet expectations."[10] I feel that this quote applies not only to marriages but to all relationships. We look to others to fill the void that only God can truly fill—the unconditional divine love of us! I am not sure if we put too much pressure and expectations on our parents, husbands, children, family, friends and co-workers, but I know that in my own life I have burned bridges because of this simple truth. We need to remember that when we genuinely *love* someone, we love their soul. Ayn Rand wrote, "Love is an expression and assertion of self-esteem, a response to one's own values in the person of another."[11] Basically, what I think she is saying is that we love a person whose core values align with our own core values and beliefs, coupled with self-love. I feel that she is only hitting the tip of the iceberg. That's not what divine love is about. For example, as a mother, I feel that the love for our children breaks all barriers and definitions of love and might come the closest to the love God has for us, his children. Don't get me wrong: as mothers we get angry, upset, and frustrated with our children, but I feel that it is easier for a mother to forgive her children than it is to forgive our parents, spouses or significant others, and other family members, friends, and coworkers.

I am going to share with you some of my own personal moments in my life when I really struggled with this truth. In my role as a mother and stepmother, I sometimes felt that God gave me a cross that I could not carry. I would ask Him, "Why, God? Why in the world did you think that I could possibly carry this burden or meet this challenge? Why do you trust me with this?" I hated myself for the negative feelings that I was having about a specific person or situation. These trials involved not just any person but a family member that I was expected to love—unconditionally. I hated it! I felt like a failure because it seemed I was betraying my God, my soul, and ultimately my purpose in life. My anger, frustration, and resentment were blinding me from the truth. I honestly detested myself because of these negative feelings. When my husband and I would agree to

---

[10] Harvey, Derek https://thoughtcatalog.com/derek-harvey/2017/11/this-is-the-silent-marriage-killer-and-its-more-deadly-than-sex-and-money/. 20 November 2017.
[11] Rand, Ayn *The Virtue of Selfishness* (Published by New American Library, New York, 1964)

disagree on certain issues, typically surrounding our different approaches to parenting—remember, we are a blended family—he would remind me that feelings are never right or wrong. They are just what they are, feelings. Throughout the years, we had learned how to handle raising six uniquely different and sometimes exceedingly difficult human beings. With that knowledge, we had to be brutally honest with each other. This honesty sometimes caused hurt feelings and at times drove a wedge in our marriage. What did we do? We prayed. We prayed hard, and we prayed together. One morning I woke up and my husband was gone. He had gone to the 6:30 a.m. mass and prayed for strength to see us through these challenges. I too prayed, and let me tell you—God always, on every single occasion, gave us clarity on the issue. His perpetual guidance is something that we can continually count on in facing the storms of life.

On one occasion, I was having difficulty with one of our children who, at the time, was making some bad life choices. This went on for quite a few years, and despite my attempts to resolve the issues and conflicts, I felt as if she was falling deeper and deeper into the *Alice's Adventures in Wonderland* rabbit hole. I could not reach down far enough to pull her out because, honestly, she did not want to come out. She liked the choices she was making, and the more I tried to force my rules on her, the further she fell down the black hole. Finally, I just prayed to God, releasing her to His grace, guidance, and protection. I was not sure what else I could do, and I felt helpless to the point that it was severely affecting my marriage. But our God is a great God, and He answered my prayers. One night while making dinner, our daughter came downstairs. I began to talk with her, really talk with her, more than I had in an exceptionally long time. I am not sure how it all happened, but I am convinced and convicted that the Holy Spirit was guiding my words. We began to talk about her upcoming confirmation and its meaning. We addressed a lot of deep topics, including Jesus being tempted by Satan in the desert and the fact that sometimes friends are not really our true friends. We talked about the fact that sometimes we are the voice of reason in certain situations, but other times our friends are the voice of reason. We need to listen to our gut and rely on our own discernment in difficult, dangerous situations, knowing that these are the moments when the Holy Spirit speaks to us. I told her that no matter what mistakes she makes or difficult situations she finds herself in, she needed to know that our home was her safe haven. And although my husband and I might be disappointed, mad, and frustrated with the choices she made, we would always unconditionally love her. The conversation lasted about an hour, and we spoke about so much more, like doing the right thing was always the hardest journey to take, but the lessons learned on that journey and the blessings that resulted in that good choice always outweighed the shortcuts of life by taking the easier route. We ended with a hug that was not just a hug, but a genuine embrace filled with love, tears, and healing. It was such a beautiful moment for me, one for which I had prayed for such a long time. This is what I am talking about here. Listen, as a mom, there are moments in life when I do not like my kids, but I always love them. They teach me as much as I teach them. This was not the last difficult situation we faced with this child of ours, nor will it be the last with any of our children, but through plugging into God as our compass, with His grace, love, and hope, we found the tools needed to navigate in the darkness of life. I have also learned that with each difficult situation, there is a hidden lesson that I need to learn. Sometimes it might involve ancestral lessons that I need to face and acknowledge to clear. Some may call it bad karma. Other times it may involve the growth and expansion of our own souls. It's like pulling back the layers of an onion. The deeper you get to the core, the more difficult it can be. You may cry, break down and yet through those break down moments, you achieve break throughs in learning more about yourself and the lesson you were meant to learn for your own soul's growth. You will not meet your true, core authentic self until you do the shadow work of peeling back your own onion skin. You have to walk in the darkness of the deep-down repressed hurts. You need to acknowledge them, feel them, and let them roll through you and then release them.

When you learn the true meaning of selfless love, it is the greatest gift that you can give to yourself and to others. I feel that this gift comes easy for some and takes time to develop for others. It is just how we are hardwired and a part of our soul's journey and growth. Some people have the ability to love, forgive, and forget much easier than others. We are all uniquely made, evidenced by the differences in the patterns found in our fingerprints. Even identical twins do not share the same fingerprints.

Motherhood taught me so much about unconditional-divine love and those experiences have molded me into the woman I am today.

The one thing I know to be unequivocally true is that you cannot love others until you first love yourself. Maybe that's part of the problem with our society. Hurting people hurt people. If you do not have love for yourself, how can you possibly have love for others? So, I guess the next question is, do you love yourself?

Love is not an emotion; love is a choice, inclusive of self-love. Love yourself! Your higher self is beckoning you to do so with all his or her might. Love yourself and forgive; forgive all your transgressions, as God loves and forgives us with unconditional grace.

CHAPTER 10

Kindness Does Matter

William Ward once wrote, "When we seek to discover the best in others, we somehow bring out the best in ourselves."[12]

Kindness does matter. We show our kindness in many ways: when we share our smiles with a stranger on the street, when we hold a door open for the next person coming through, and when we help an elderly person with their groceries. I could go on and on, but we all know that these small acts of kindness make a difference in this world. Sometimes giving kindness is hardest with those we love the best. We allow our frustrations, annoyances, anger, and resentment to build up, and it affects our kindness meter. These are the moments when we are tested. It is not how we behave in the spotlight that matters or when it is just easy to be nice on the days when we just happen to be in a good mood. Kindness matters in the shadows where no one else can see, when you know that you are doing the right thing. Kindness matters in those moments when it is hard to be kind and on those tough days when being kind takes every ounce of your being, but you do it anyway because it is the right thing to do. If you do not have anything nice to say, silence is golden. If you hear gossip about someone else, keep it to yourself unless it may be harmful to the safety of others. The principle I try to stand on is, "If it's not my story to tell, I won't tell it." Think about how you interact with others. Are there

---

[12] William Arthur Ward - When we seek to discover the best in... (brainyquote.com)

people to whom you could be kinder? Are there people whom you have treated poorly but honestly do not have a real reason for your unkindness? Take some time to reflect and try to be a kinder person. As my dad would say, "It's a beautiful thing." Two of the sweetest people in my life are my sister-in-law Maricel and my cousin Trish. I am grateful to not only call them family but also call them my tribe sisters.

Princess Diana said, "Carry out a random act of kindness, with no expectation of reward, safe in the knowledge that one day someone might do the same for you."[13] You can get the exact same point across with an authoritative stance, anger, harsh and hurtful words, domination, power, control and destruction as you can with a kind tone. You can choose love to get your point across. Loving expressions come with grace, understanding, and kind empowering words! If you were on the receiving end of your words, how would you feel? Really think about that. Would you feel encouraged and empowered, or would you feel defeated and defensive? What type of person are you? Do you really like being that person? If you did not choose the *loving* choice, then, I'm so sorry to tell you my friend, you need to find some self-meditation time because you have some shadow work that you need to clear. For many, these issues are directly connected to low self-esteem and self-confidence, which equates to self-worth. We all have the power to change ourselves into better versions, so do not feel defeated. When I was a Mary Kay Independent Sales Director, I was told that Mary Kay Ash always believed, "We all have an invisible sign on our back stating, 'Make me feel special, make me feel important.'"[14] You too have this sign on your back. Be inclusive and not exclusive when dealing with others. Can you imagine if the hurt you do to others was given to your own child? How differently would you behave? Be the love and light of God. Choose to be the best version of you.

[13] Princess of Wales, Diana. "Princess Diana Quotes." *Brainy Quotes.* 2001. https://www.brainyquote.com/quotes/princess_diana_154326
[14] Ash, Mary Kay. "Miracles Happen." 2003. Quill, New York.

CHAPTER 11

Being a Good Communicator

What is communication? It's an exchange of thoughts, opinions, and information. This exchange happens through our speech, writing and through signs. Communication is so vitally important in life. You need to learn how to be a clear, conscientious, honest communicator in every aspect of your life. You need to find your authentic voice and not be afraid to use it. Remember that when you speak out of frustration, anger, or resentment (your lower energy ego-self), your words may come across as harsh, hurtful, and mean. When you are feeling like this, do not be afraid to take a time-out for yourself so you can process those emotions first and respond afterward. Be proactive and not reactive. Our words can act like arrows, piercing the hearts of others, or they can be used with love. "Reckless words pierce like a sword, but the tongue of the wise brings healing" (Proverbs 12:18).

Your words can be a double-edged sword. You can pierce others, and you can pierce yourself. Watch your own self-talk. Be your own biggest fan. Be careful with your words. Be exquisite, flawless, immaculate, precise, infallible, accurate, and unblemished with your words. Be authentic and genuine, and be the truth of light and love with every word you use.

Along the lines of communication, the next topic includes our assumptions. Never make assumptions in life. As the saying goes, "When you assume, you make an ass out of you and me." Instead of assuming, ask. Use communication to clarify a situation or circumstance. Many times, you will discover that your initial thoughts were not correct. It is always better to err on the side of caution. This is also the case when dealing with gossip. When you hear something that does not line up with the previous knowledge and experiences you have with that other person, take time to find out the truth. If it does not sound or feel like the truth, it most likely is not. Do not further the gossip and follow others when you know that the situation is not lining up with what you know about the person being discussed. If the situation does not involve you, then remember your role and stay in your own lane. My motto has always been, "If it is not my story to tell, I am not telling it to others."

If the situation involves you, then take the time to stop and question things. The biblical principle directs us to take it to the source for truth and clarification. Ask the person directly. This should also be our practice when dealing with an argument or misunderstanding with another person. Instead of gossiping and talking to everyone else about the situation, take it to the source. You will find that when you do this, you will most likely work things out and gain the respect of the other person by handling it the right way.

We, as humans, tend to twist situations into the best light for ourselves. Even when we are trying to be honest, it is human nature to take our own side or the side of the person whom we love the best or know the best. But when dealing with "he said, she said" situations, remember that there are always three sides: his side, her side, and the truth.

I think I have mentioned this before, but it bears repeating. One of the top reasons for failed relationships is unmet expectations. We can only express our own expectations through communication, and we can only know the expectations of others by asking.

Being a good communicator involves listening—not just listening but hearing and processing what the other person is telling you. Sometimes this involves repeating what you think you heard to make sure you heard it correctly. You have most likely heard this before: we have two ears and one mouth for a reason. We should listen twice as much as we speak. When we communicate, we want others to actively listen to us without interruption, and in turn we owe that same consideration and respect to others. When I was in Sedona, Arizona, for a spiritual retreat, I was able to spend half of a day with a Native American named Crystal Moon. That day brought me so much clarity and light on the shadow side of my own soul yet was balanced with the spiritual gifts that I bring to this world. It was such an emotional day filled with such light, love, self-love, and self-healing through my shadow work. Crystal reminded me that I need to take a step back and stand firmly in my silence. When I did, I found the whisper of my higher self, from God. In my silence, I allow myself to listen to the stories of others without mentally preparing my response, without judging, and without becoming defensive, which is a part of my ego-self. She also taught me that I no longer need to use the words, "I'm sorry." I can instead use the words "oops" or express gratitude in the place of apology. For example, I can say "Thank you for your patience with me" instead of "I'm sorry I'm late." As an empath, I like to help, but Crystal also reminded me that I am not a healer or a helper. Rather, I am a channel for healing light frequencies to connect with those in need, who must be open to this energy. Therefore, I am not a helper but rather an aide, an assistant, a supporter in their own journeys. If you're ever in Sedona, Arizona, you should look her up. I promise you it will be a magical spiritual experience.

In certain circumstances you will find yourself feeling like a dog chasing its tail, meaning that you and another person may have to agree to disagree. When you find yourself in these moments, do not forget that your silence can be the best answer. In certain situations, silence is golden.

Other times you will find yourself feeling such attunement with another person, almost as if you are one with him or her. It is a feeling that goes beyond listening. It is the kinesthetic knowing that occurs when we allow our inner state of being to resonate with that of another. Many couples, twin flames, or soul mates achieve this form of connection and intimacy. It can also develop in friendships.

One last thing I would like to suggest about communication is to have an open mind to learn new words daily. Every day I receive an email from the Word Genius website[15] with a new word; the words are from different origins, from all over the world. It provides me with the correct pronunciation and definition. It is super cool. I'm continually working on using these words throughout my day to broaden my own personal vocabulary, and so should we all.

We also should work on looking through the mirror of life, allowing access to another person's point of view or stepping into the shoes of others. When we experience this shift in perspective, looking at the other side, we open ourselves up and allow our own minds to experience new realms of existence. It provides a platform for learning about different worlds, cultures, heritages, and religions, which can lead to understanding. Understanding can lead to acceptance, love, appreciation, and respect of others. Isn't that a better option for personal growth? Do not allow yourself to fall back into the trap of being defensive or judgmental just because you do not understand the other point of view. When you remain in opposition, you remain in attack mode, and nothing ever gets accomplished with that approach.

---

[15] Word Genius https://www.wordgenius.com

CHAPTER 12

Perspective

*P*erspective is a particular attitude toward or way of regarding something, a point of view. It has a Latin root that means "look through" or "perceive." Perspective is a funny thing. When you learn to appreciate another person's perspective, you open your mind to learn and grow. In life you will discover that the answers to many of life's mysteries are found in shades of gray, meaning that there is not just one correct answer. It is perspective. I find it beautiful when my children see something differently than I do and explain their perspective. Learn to appreciate the unique differences with each person who enters your life. Open yourself up to their perspective. Perspective can also be thought of as your personal truth. We all choose to stand in our truths and live out our own stories. Individual perspectives and truths vary from person to person. Knowing this will help you sustain your solid foundation and walk in your own truth without crossing into someone else's truth. It is knowing your role and staying in your own lane without self-judgment or judgment of others. You do not have to change your point of view by giving respect for another person's point of view. When you find yourself in a situation of agreeing to disagree, stop yourself and just listen. Look at the issues as if walking in their shoes and be respectful of their journey. You might not agree, but you do not have to because their truth is really none of your business. When you can open yourself up to this wisdom, you just might find that you have learned something extremely useful on your own truth journey. When others cannot handle your truth just remind yourself that you can hold compassion and empathy as they experience their own reactions to your truth. There is never a need to apologize when standing in your own truth and perspective.

CHAPTER 13

Being Good Enough

In life, we have all had those moments of great victory, basking in the glory of being on top of the world. This may have happened when you were younger, at one of your Little League games, at a dance competition, at a science fair, or in your high school football league championship game. Maybe it did not happen to you until college, when you got that 4.0 GPA that you had strived to achieve for many years. Maybe it did not happen until adulthood, landing that dream job, getting the much-desired promotion, or landing the big account. Maybe you have not yet had your big victory, yet you can feel, taste, see, and smell that moment of victory beckoning you from beyond the horizon.

In these great moments of life, you feel so alive, yet as humans, we tend to forget this euphoric feeling quickly, which leaves us questioning, "Am I good enough?" We sometimes feel disappointed with ourselves because we don't have the careers we want, we don't make the money we think we deserve, we don't have the houses of our dreams, or we don't drive the cars that we desire. When we do this to ourselves, those negative thoughts wreak havoc on our mental psyche. Negative thoughts are like a festering cancer, a silent killer. They deaden the mind and weaken the heart, which leads us to settle in the midst of our own mediocrity. We must first believe that we are not only good enough but better than enough. The mind is such a powerful, underutilized tool. The brain is a complex organ filled with one hundred billion neurons carrying information from cell to cell. According to neurologist Barry Gordon, "Most of our brain is always active and is even active while in resting or sleep mode."[16] There is a myth that we only use 10 percent of our brains, which is a perpetuated urban legend. The truth is that we use our entire brains, both hemispheres, and this raises the question of how we can maximize the use and full potential of our brains. What are we feeding our minds? When we focus on negative thoughts like *I am not good enough*, our brains cannot perform at a high or even normal capacity. It has been proven that the more you focus on negativity, the more neurons your brain will create that support your negative thoughts. Such thoughts slow down the brain's ability to function, which can lead to depression and anxiety. On the flip side, positive thinking can truly lead to happiness, which leads to better stress-coping skills and then to greater success in life. I love the motto "What you think about, you bring about." Positive thinking not only changes the way we behave, but it also encourages those around us to become better people. You can train your brain for happiness and success, but it requires a keen awareness of your daily self-talk, and it definitely takes time to transition from negativity to positivity, from "Am I good enough?" to "I'm great!" Believe me, this is still a struggle for me. Despite the knowledge that I have, I find myself slipping into negative self-talk, which leads to feeling upset, angry, and bitter. When I give in to this negativity, I am giving my negative thoughts the power over my mind. In these moments, I tell myself, "Cancel, cancel, cancel," and I try to look at the positive in each situation. I have had numerous moments of not feeling good enough in my career and in my personal life as a daughter, sister, wife, mother, stepmother, and friend. You will have people in your life journey who will try to tear you down to your bitter core and make you question your own existence. Do not let them! Remember, our minds were designed to be blank canvases, colored with the positive emotions within our authentic hearts. What a beautiful canvas you are. Take a step back and look at your tribe, the character of your people. Reclaim your power and authority. You are the coauthor of your own story. I honestly feel that we can discover a lot about who we are just by looking at the groups of our core tribes. Our core tribes may include family members

[16] Boyd, Robynne. https://www.scientificamerican.com/article/do-people-only-use-10-percent-of-their-brains/. 2 February 2008.

and "lifer" friends. If your close family members and friends exhibit the traits of being genuine people of good character with high morals and ethics, you can be certain that you too possess those positive prosocial traits. How do you discern real friends from false ones? Real friends are painfully and honestly direct to your face but say nice things behind your back, while false friends say nice things about you to your face but say painful things behind your back. I am grateful that I have so many true soul-tribe people in my life because they have provided support, guidance, and love during some difficult times with my own life. I am grateful for the people who have been woven into my career path. These people provide opportunities for my continued personal and professional growth. I am just as much a part of your success, as you are to mine!

If you find yourself looking at your tribe and thinking, *I don't have any of these people in my life*, then pray and get into action. I promise that God will not let you down; you will find them because He will put them on your life path. God will answer your prayers. He always does.

While I was going through my divorce, a beautiful friend of mine, Melissa, bought me a magnet. It was a simple gift, but I will forever cherish it because of the simple quote, which I read daily for many years, as it got me through some of my toughest days. The magnet said, "Never be content with someone else's definition of you." When you choose to be the cocreator, you define who you are and who you will become, and in that moment, you take back control of your own destiny. You are the author of your own book. If you do not like how the story is going, then change it. The great news is that you have the power; you are wearing the magical red slippers. You can unlearn counterproductive beliefs and thoughts and replace them with positive productive thoughts. It all starts with a decision each morning as you wake up to start your day. We need to hold onto the moments of victory, relive past moments of success, and know that we can achieve a multitude of new, positive victorious moments in our lives because we are good enough. I hope that you find friends who remind you of this, like my friend Marlene.

CHAPTER 14

Marlene, My Other Mother

My beautiful, eloquent, wise, fun-loving friend, old-soul Marlene, and I met when I was only twenty-three. I had been hired as a judicial aide at one of the local district courts in the metropolitan area of Detroit. I was still wet behind the ears, as some say. I met Marlene, and she was one of those people who come into your life that you are eternally grateful for. She took me under her wings and taught me so much about life, love, hardship, and survival, as well as how to take dire situations and turn them into life lessons. She had that dry sense of humor that not many people understand, but I did. She was my mama bear at work. She looked out for me and still does. She is one of the people I can call at any given moment, and she would drop whatever she was doing to come to my aide—spiritually, emotionally, physically, and financially. She will never take any credit for the blessings and gifts that she provides to others because she is too humble, but I will tell you that she is one of my diamond friends. I love her with all my heart and soul. Her wisdom, insight, and discernment of life continues to provide me with support on my own life journey. She is a beacon of light, love, laughter, understanding, wisdom, and wit. For these reasons, I had to add her to this book. I love you, Marlene! You are a beautiful soul. I hope you have your own version of Marlene in your life. Her actions always made me feel more than good enough.

CHAPTER 15

Quit Comparing Yourself to Others

I know you have heard this before, but it bears repeating: when you compare yourself to others, you are comparing their absolute best to your very worst, their strengths to your weaknesses. Why do we do this to ourselves? Do you really know what is going on in other people's lives? Maybe they have their own struggles, pain, sadness, tragedy, and heartache, yet you do not know because they do not broadcast it to others. You really can't tell what is going on in anyone else's life but your own; all you see is the beautiful red silk ribbon and the perfectly wrapped present, not what's really going on inside the cardboard box.

My friend Lisa refers to Facebook as "Fakebook." With that she reminds me that, as humans, we always want to put our best foot forward, meaning that most of us share the highlights of our lives and not the darkness.

Quit comparing yourself to others. Doing so is one of the most damaging mental games that you play with yourself. It took me an exceedingly long time to learn this truth, and honestly, sometimes it is simply hard not to compare.

The best advice that I can give you when you find yourself in the mind trap is to completely remove yourself from the equation. Just be happy for the other person—I mean, genuinely happy. Feel their joy and share in the happiness. The more you give of yourself and of your love, the more you will receive. Embrace your uniqueness. God designed you perfectly for your destiny, so please embrace the beauty of that truth. Once you learn this lesson, you will feel better about yourself and your life path, which only you were designed to travel. When you have this mindset, it also changes your thought patterns toward others and allows a natural flow of love and happiness so you can truly be happy for other people's blessings. Do not make permanent decisions with temporary emotions about yourself.

CHAPTER 16

Don't Take Things Personally

This has always been one of the hardest life lessons that I have struggled with. Remember that those other people's opinions, beliefs, actions, and reactions are theirs, not yours. Consider the serenity prayer: "God, grant me the serenity to accept the things I cannot change, courage to change the things I can, and wisdom to know the difference."[17] When you learn not to take anything personally, you will release so much hurt, tension, stress, and anxiety from your life.

The Dalai Lama advised, "We often add to our pain and suffering by being overly sensitive, overreacting to minor things, and sometimes taking things too personally."[18]

Ah, sweet, sweet sensitivity. Why do others look at it as a weakness when I feel that it is such a grounding strength? Being in tune and aligned with your emotions is such a spiritual gift. To know your own emotions is to know your own soul. To know another's emotion is the key to life. Connection, empathy, and understanding create a bridge from our selfish ego-selves to our true spiritual-selves, which is giving of our own love

[17] Littleton, Jeanett Gardner; Bell, James Stuart (2008). Living the Serenity Prayer: True Stories of Acceptance, Courage, and Wisdom. Avon, Massachusetts: Adams Media. p. 14. ISBN 978-1-59869-116-0.
[18] Dalai Lama (2009). "The Art of Happiness, 10th Anniversary Edition: A Handbook for Living", p.112, Riverhead Books, Penguin Group, New York 2009

and light to others in need of the healing that we can provide through our understanding. If you remove your sensitivity, you remove the very essence of who you are. Being aware of our own feelings and having a deep awareness of the feelings of others provides us the spiritual gifts of our conscious awareness of empathy, intuition, and creativity, which allows us to reach out and influence other lives.

For you sensitive souls, hold onto that gift and remind yourself that your personal self-worth is never attached to someone else's opinion of you. Their opinion of you is not any of your business. The one thing that we can always take control of is our own thoughts, which ultimately leads to our actions. Although many people have hidden agendas, we must not fall into that mindset and become like them. Instead, we must lean on the Lord for guidance and direction. "Create in me a clean heart, O God, and renew a steadfast spirit within me" (Psalm 51:10).

Author L. R. Knost says, "Do not be dismayed by the brokenness of the world. All things break. And all things can be mended. Not with time, as they say, but with intention. So, go, love intentionally, extravagantly, unconditionally. The broken world waits in darkness for the light that is you."[19]

The ultimate goal is finding the balance of maintaining your sensitivity yet not taking things personally. Sometimes it may feel like walking on a tightrope, but when you wrap your field of protective power around yourself, you can maintain your selfless, empathic nature without being drained and hurt by your ego-self.

---

[19] L.K. Knost: Two Thousand Kisses a Day: Gentle Parenting Through the Ages and Stages." 20 February 2013.

CHAPTER 17

The Difference between Being Ordinary and Being Extraordinary

"The difference between ordinary and extraordinary is always found in your daily discipline." I have said this phrase repeatedly throughout the years to my children as they have developed from children to teens to adults and through their adulthood. I've said it so much that, as soon as I begin it, I hear a heavy sigh, hear "Oh, Mom," or see the infamous eye roll. Despite their sighs, comments, and eye rolls, they know in their hearts that it is true.

In life, you cannot expect great results if you are not willing to put in your best while achieving your goals. We have all had those moments when we thought we were giving our best, but deep within the depths of our souls, we knew that we could and should be giving more. Now that I am older and reflect on my life, I regret not living by this motto of greatness in all areas of my life, especially in my earlier years. I know that I took many learning opportunities for granted. Now I try to focus every day to become more keenly aware of the opportunities put before me. They are flowing around each of us all the time. The key is making the time to stop, listen, and learn. We all have the same 24 hours, 1,440 minutes, and 86,400 seconds every day, yet how many of us waste this precious commodity of time on negative thoughts and activities that don't propel us into becoming the great people God designed us to be?

One of the best ways to learn and grow and go from ordinary to extraordinary is by learning from our elders. They have a lot of life experience under their belts, and if we take the time to stop and listen to their stories, we can learn so much. History, whether it's good, bad, or ugly, is there for us to learn from. With that knowledge, we can make better decisions within our own lives. Those who choose to turn away from history or the wisdom of our elders have chosen to relearn those lessons, a decision that takes them down a difficult and long road.

I am going to share a story with you about Leo, who was an immigrant from Italy. I met him when a group of my friends and our husbands got together to play boccie ball at a local Italian American Club, in Livonia, Michigan, one cold February night. As we were getting our teams together on the boccie lanes and learning the rules of the game, we made our best attempts to throw the pallino boccie balls down the lane. I noticed three older, Italian-looking chaps watching from the distance, and I heard one of them laugh as he left the building. Leo was not one of them. He walked over to me and my friends, introduced himself, and asked if we would like some pointers on how to play the game, and of course we took him up on his offer. He was a very snappy dresser and wore an Italian flat cap. He really was adorable, and boy, could he play boccie ball. He was there with his family, celebrating his sister-in-law's birthday. While his wife and the other ladies were playing cards at a nearby table, Leo stayed and watched us play boccie. After the tournament was over, my husband walked over to the wall-sized photo of Italy and noticed the hundreds of names of various villages and cities listed on it, which led to his conversation with Leo. Leo's father had left his family when he was young, and at the age of sixteen, he had to move away to obtain employment to help his mother and siblings with the bills. He moved to a few different countries on his journey but ended up in Detroit, Michigan. Within a few years, he brought over his brother and his sister, and he and his brother learned the art of breadmaking at a bakery in Detroit. Because Leo was a man with extraordinary drive, he took the time to learn how to bake bread. Years later, he opened his own bakery in the town I grew up in, Garden City. Realizing the connection from my youth and the great memories of this bakery, I ended up talking with Leo about his life journey and was in awe of his drive, determination, and passion.

He was in his mid-eighties, but you would have never guessed it because he still had that youthful sparkle in his eyes as he shared his stories with us and I shared with him my love for his bakery. It was not just any bakery; it was an Italian bakery with decadent butter cookies, homemade pasta and breads, and the best stuffed pizza bread you will ever have. I still love going to that bakery and have taken my own children there to experience the goodness of their Italian pizza bread. Leo is just one example of how you can go from having an ordinary life to having an extraordinary life and building a legacy. Every Garden City High School student still knows about Villa Bakery. Although he sold the business, his authentic recipes can still be purchased from the bakery today.

I try to give 150 percent of myself in every situation. I said this once to a friend, and he responded, "That's impossible! You can only give 100 percent." I disagreed with him because I feel that you can reach beyond 100 percent. Honestly, how else do we grow? It is like our expanding universe, which has been growing since the big bang. I must be honest with you: I am not the most disciplined person, but my husband is. He is a prime example of how to apply discipline to your life to catapult to the next level. When he was a young boy, he played basketball, and because he grew so rapidly, he had difficulty learning how to control his new lanky body. Yet he was determined to overcome this obstacle because he wanted to be the best. He did not just think about it or talk about it; he practiced each day on the little cement basketball slab his dad built for him. His mom and dad told me that he would practice for hours and hours on the mini basketball court, even in the dark. When he felt confident enough in his skills, he began to play with the older boys in his neighborhood because he knew that would be the only way to grow as a player. He ended up injuring his knee and had to stop playing, but when he entered high school, he took up football. Once again, he was not the most naturally talented player on the field, but his "never give up, never give in" attitude earned him recognition in high school. His success led to his receiving a couple of college football scholarships, one of them to Hillsdale College in Hillsdale, Michigan, known for its exceptional academic program. There, he earned his undergraduate degree and moved on to obtain his master's degree in special education from Wayne State University in Detroit.

He is now an eighth-grade history teacher who shares his passion for football through his coaching at the high school level. In 2019, the year I began this book, he was nominated and honored with the city award of Middle School Teacher of the Year. Although he is my husband, I honestly do not know anyone more deserving of this award. He gets up at four to five each morning to start his day, and many days he does not get home until eight or nine at night. He pours everything he has into his passion for teaching his students and coaching his players. He spearheaded the eighth-grade Washington D.C. and Philadelphia trip and serves as the lead teacher for the Civil War days experience, which is a week-long interactive program for the eighth-grade students at his school. He also organizes the Thanksgiving food baskets for families in need within the Livonia, Michigan community. His State of Michigan Special Tribute says that he is known for his "coach" personality and teaching style, allowing his enthusiasm and passion for teaching students the history of the United States to shine through. He believes in establishing an environment of trust, safety, respect, responsibility, and learning. He invests in his students and ensures that those with various learning styles can thrive in his teaching environment. He is a selfless person who leads by example and truly is an exceptional human. I am grateful that our worlds collided because, through his daily actions, he certainly brings out the best in me. You should check out his Twitter account, @Fryguyhistory.[20]

You will never know the full potential of greatness that lies inside of you until you choose to be great. Greatness is achieved by giving 150 percent of yourself—heart, mind, body, and soul—in everything you do. Do not worry about the results; it is the process of growth that should be your number one concern. God's timing for us may not always align with our own personal timelines, and that's OK because divine timing is perfection. Life is not about the destination; it truly is about the journey and the souls that join you on this amazing ride.

So what are you waiting for? Go be extraordinary!

---

[20] Fryer Matthew @fryguyhistory Twitter

CHAPTER 18

Train the Excellent in You

How do you train the excellent in you? Who are you surrounding yourself with? What are you reading? What are you watching on TV, the internet, and YouTube? To achieve your full potential, I think you need to be well-rounded. What do I mean by that? Think of it as a pie with different slices containing the following elements: social, spiritual, emotional, environmental, occupational, intellectual, physical, and financial.

Two of my sons participated in karate, specifically Tang Soo Do Moo Duk Kwan. I remember watching my sons practice at the dojo. One day, I really took a moment to read the words posted on the walls. Thank you, Master John Prosch, for your commitment, dedication, and love of the art and the children you trained.

Personal Development Creed:

1. Be a leader, not a follower.
2. Think positively, and positive things will happen.
3. Socialize with positive, goal-oriented peers like yourself.
4. Develop the courage to stand up for yourself and do what is right.
5. Keep yourself physically and mentally fit.
6. Be truthful and just in all that you do.
7. Focus on your schoolwork and drive yourself to overachieve.

8. Help your parents without being asked.
9. Give priority to the things that can help you be a success in life.
10. Practice, practice, practice leads to mastery.

Goal-Setting Creed:

1. Visualize your goal, then write it down.
2. Who can help you?
3. What are the obstacles?
4. When will your goal be accomplished?
5. Where will your goal be achieved?
6. Why do you want to achieve this goal?
7. How will you achieve this goal?
8. Avoid procrastination and understand failure.

It takes discipline to chisel away at yourself and uncover the true potential and beauty of who you are. It is a process that takes time. Be loving and patient with yourself. Do you know the story of Michelangelo's astonishing creation of the statue of David? It is so beautiful! The story is that Michelangelo was only twenty-six years old yet already the most famous artist in his day. He accepted a challenge from Arte della Lana, who had commissioned a series of twelve large Old Testament sculptures for the buttress of the cathedral, to sculpt a large-scale David. Many were contracted before Michelangelo, but none had his vision. While walking in Carrara, Italy, one day, Michelangelo noticed a huge piece of marble. It had been on this very same path he had walked for years, yet with perfect divine timing, he finally saw it. As he looked at it, his mind's eye was able to form the vision of his future masterpiece. Within the solid block of marble, he found what he was searching for. He began the masterpiece in 1501 and completed it in 1504. For those of you who have not seen it, close your eyes and visualize the details that I am about to describe to you. Michelangelo's *David* was chiseled with fixed, strong, yet watchful eyes; pulsing veins on the back of his hand; and such defined beauty of the male physique, from the taut torso to his flexing thigh muscles and from the top of his curled locks to the bottoms of his grounded feet. To see this magnificent creation would send a lightning bolt of energy up and down your spine.

Michelangelo worked day and night, despite the rainy and cold weather. At the end of those years of creation, he completed the masterpiece that we all know as *David*. In January 1504, his fourteen-feet-tall *David* was unveiled, and to honor the perfection of his sculpture, the commission decided to place the piece behind Santa Maria del Fiore Cathedral in the Piazza della Signoria. It took four days and forty men to move the statue a half a mile to its resting place in Signoria Square on June 8th. David was the symbol of liberty and freedom of the Republican ideals, supporting Florence's readiness to defend itself during that time in history.

Have you ever wanted something so much? Something that consumes every ounce of your being that you had to make it happen? I have on multiple occasions, as I think we all have. The difference is that some of us, like me, want it now!

I am a Scorpio. We Scorpios are passionate, and although we are a fixed sign, when we fixate on what we want, *patience* is not a word we want to hear. We have difficulty in the waiting phase. I am not saying that this phase does not include action, because it does. But we have difficulty knowing that it is not necessarily going to happen on our timeline.

I admire those who have patience, like Michelangelo—the patience to work yet wait, to sit patiently in the journey of accomplishment, achievement, and completion of that goal. As I've said previously, God doesn't call the equipped, but He does equip the called, which means that the lessons we learn on the journey, while climbing the ladder toward our goal, are truly part of the goal itself. We need to learn to take the time to chisel and sculpt ourselves because we are all magnificent masterpieces, too precious to rush the process of completion. We must find our vision and move into action while embracing the journey to claim our prize, which is the completion of our goal. That completion is part of our defined life journeys, part of our destinies. When God places a vision in your heart and mind, it is yours to claim. But you must first be willing to take the action required to achieve your goal. This takes great work ethic, perseverance, and patience. When you put that wheel into action, that journey will lead you to the goals you have set for yourself. That moment of victory, when you get to embrace the reward that you have worked so hard to achieve, is the moment you claim your prize and feel that state of complete balance and harmony.

In reflecting on this chapter so far, I realized I would be remiss if I didn't include the story of my uncle Harry Fryer Jr., a.k.a. Uncle Buck. He is my husband's paternal uncle, and he was stricken with polio at the mere age of six years old. Despite the limited medical knowledge at that time, he surpassed any limitations that were placed on him due to his disease. He is the most mentally and spiritually advanced soul I have met in this lifetime. As I was completing this book, he reached his ninety-fifth birthday. He is of sound mind and soul, never forgetting any of our children's birthdays, and he shares so many of his life stories with such detail that I am amazed. As a younger man, he refused to receive any public assistance, worked his entire life, and was a self-taught sailing and CPR instructor. He would travel in his specially equipped van in summers, traveling up and down the coasts of Michigan to sail on his own. He is such an amazing soul. He would make each of us question whether or not we are survivors or victims of our circumstances. I absolutely love you UB! What an inspiration you are to us all.

PART 3
Who Are You?

As I reflect on this topic, the starfish comes to mind. What I love about the starfish is its ability to renew and regenerate itself. Starfish are celestial symbols, representing infinite divine love.

Photographed by Ana F. Fryer

CHAPTER 19

Who Are You Socially?

I read this intention to myself every day: "I use exceptionally great communication skills to attract positive, prosocial people into my life who motivate me to become the best version of myself I can be."

When my kids were younger and into their teens, I tried to help guide them to select good friends because positive breeds positive and negative breeds negative. We humans pick up the vibes, beliefs, traits, attitudes, mindsets, and verbiage of those with whom we surround ourselves. Whether you want to admit it or not, your close family, friends, and coworkers influence the choices that you make in life, so you need to choose wisely. Your friendship circle reflects you. Choose wisely.

When I met my second husband, one of the many traits that I fell in love with was his ability to make me a better version of myself. He inspires me. He challenges me. He supports me. He helped me find the best in myself. Our visions and goals are in alignment, and I think that we complement one another. I am the yin to his yang. There is a balance and completion with him in my life.

You want to find people who are supportive, loving, caring, ambitious, inspiring, and creative yet can be heartfully honest with you. When you find these types of people in your life, hold onto them, cherish them, and appreciate them.

As you grow, you will find that your circle will change. Sometimes you will have to let go, and sometimes you will need to add. When you let go of someone, do not stop loving, but learn to love from a distance. Some people are energy takers, and they will empty your cup. You need to let them go or learn to distance yourself for protection. Do not be afraid to step out of your comfort zone to meet new people. Join a new gym, church, or community group. Don't ever hesitate to step outside the comfort of your circle to reach higher and find those earth angels who will fill your cup and lift you to a higher level. Because let's face it—you were really meant to fly. When you have a full cup, it will naturally overflow and affect others. A waterfall of your life, love, and light is what the Hokey Pokey is all about (thank you, Mom and Dad, for that awesome analogy). Making a difference in others' lives and adding value to others brings fulfillment to the core of your soul. The blessing is that the more you give, the more you receive. What an amazing truth!

CHAPTER 20

Who Are You Spiritually?

The intention I read to myself every day is, "I live at a higher level of vibration, and I know my core values and beliefs, while continually reaching to grow my spirituality daily." We all believe in something. Even believing in nothing is believing in something—it is just nothing. Discover your higher power of belief and plug into it. A higher power of belief is one based on pure love, kindness, and gentleness for all humankind. Any power in contrast to that is not a healthy belief for yourself or others around you. When you tap into your authentic self, your true self, your soul, you will begin your own true spiritual journey. In our world of information and stimulation overload, it is hard to find the time to quiet your space, calm your mind, and let your soul speak to you. Make a conscious effort to make time—just like you make the time to shower, brush your teeth, eat, and sleep—for your spiritual growth. Find the time to make yourself the priority, and your true self will speak to you loud and clear.

For me, dance was one of my spiritual outlets. When I heard a song, I would begin to mentally choreograph and lose myself in the moment. It would take me to a higher frequency level. I know it might sound crazy, but now that I am older, my shower time is when I can find time to meditate and pray. It is when my mind flows freely, and when I am done, I feel not only physically cleansed on the outside but spiritually renewed on the inside. When you find the time to allow your spiritual self to flow through you, you will find your authentic self. Be aware of that time because it is different for each of us, and tap into it. Really take time to spend with yourself. Allow yourself to check out of the crazy mayhem of life and just be. We are in a constant struggle between our ego-selves and the duality of this third-dimensional world versus our soul-selves and the neutral perspective of the fourth- and fifth dimensional worlds.[21]

Following are some other spiritual lessons posted on my son's dojo.

The Articles of Faith:

1. Be loyal to your country. (I would add *to what you believe in and stand for*)
2. Be obedient to your parents. (I would add *respectful*)
3. Be lovable between husband and wife. (I would add *your partner)*
4. Be cooperative between brothers. (I would add *sisters/all humanity*)
5. Be faithful between friends.
6. Be respectful to your elders.
7. Be faithful between teacher and student.
8. Know the difference between good and evil.
9. Never retreat in battle. (I would add that you can *stand your ground*)
10. Always finish what you start.

Meditation and yoga are two other great ways to quiet your soul, channel your inner voice, and connect to your higher power. Through these two activities, you can reconnect with your true self. In life, our identities can get lost or tucked away because we all have an innate desire to be loved and accepted, which can sometimes lead to our wearing masks, literally (thank you, COVID-19) and figuratively, to hide our true selves. Sometimes we feel that we need to change who we really are for the acceptance of others. When this happens, we pretend to be someone we are not to fit in and be accepted, but we do not need to sacrifice our souls to find this true love and acceptance. Take the time to spend with

---

[21] Ladd, Lorie. 8 June 2020. YouTube Video Channel Lorie Ladd. "Ascending Now: Interview with Arielle Caputo & Lorie Ladd. Https://LorieLadd.com.

yourself in reflection to reconnect with your true, authentic self. You *don't* have to be loved by everyone. Because I am an empath, this has been a struggle for me throughout life. An empath takes on the emotional states of others. For years, I did not know or understand this. I would find myself in situations where I felt extremely emotional and felt that I was responsible for the safety, happiness, and well-being of others because I was absorbing other people's emotions. Only later in life did I understand the meaning of being an empath and discover that I am highly sensitive to other people's emotions. Being intuitive and psychic, I had to learn how to protect myself from other people's moods, good or bad. Through yoga and meditation and becoming a Reiki master, I have learned how to find the balance of loving and supporting those around me while also protecting myself from absorbing the negativity, anger, or anxiety of others. Empaths are naturally giving spirits, which can lead an empath to feelings of vulnerability and hurt. Too much togetherness can be difficult for empaths, so they need time alone. Being so highly connected to the energies of others can lead to exhaustion. Empaths are targets for "energy vampires," such as narcissists, who make empaths feel unworthy and unlovable. Such interactions can be physically and emotionally draining, and therefore empaths need to learn strategies to survive and protect their power from energy takers or excessive noise. Because empaths have huge hearts, they often give too much of themselves as they try to ease the pain of others. They may find themselves drawn into situations that don't involve them because of their sensitivity to others, which leads to distress. Once I learned the skills of time management, setting boundaries and limits, finding solitude, meditating, and doing yoga, I stopped feeling overloaded by guilt, depression, anger, resentment from others and learned how to ground and reconnect to my true self. Being an empath is a gift that I do cherish, but if you too are an empath, you need to honor yourself and your true spirit and learn how to protect your power.

CHAPTER 21

Who Are You Financially?

Oh, I love this question! I want to first start off by stating that financial abundance is personal and looks different for each of us. Some people find financial abundance through living a simple life while others may find it through living an extravagant lifestyle. I was told at an incredibly young age that I was middle class and that was all I was going to be. It felt constraining to me and I felt as if this false belief was passed down from my parents, grandparents, and so on. When I was younger, I often heard, "We can't afford it" and "We don't have enough money." I ended up doing this exact same thing to my own children, especially after my divorce. I remember taking back my parents' returnable pop bottles and turning in loose change just to get groceries for the week. We lived on a very tight budget. Natalie, my oldest, heard me say, "We can't afford it" the most. As I got back on my feet with the help of promotions in my criminal justice career and the financial benefit of having two incomes after my second marriage, my financial situation improved. Yet that false belief that I did not deserve or could not have the abundant lifestyle I wanted lingered. I discovered later in life that I could control the answer to the question "Who am I financially?" and learned how to manifest abundance in all areas of my life. This transformation did not occur overnight, and honestly, I catch myself falling back on those limiting beliefs. In achieving this change, I had to figure out how to deprogram myself from those negative ancestral beliefs and the generational programs that had been imprinted upon me by my own parents at such a young age. These limiting beliefs about money, wealth, abundance, and worthiness had to be replaced by thoughts that were more aligned with my authentic self. I'm proud to say that my children have learned from my experiences of this false belief. They have abundant bank accounts and beliefs within themselves that they can achieve whatever they want in life without living in the archaic trap of financial debt, as many of our families did. They have learned that they do *not* have to give their power away to various institutional systems that, on the surface, appear to be an avenue of assistance, yet actually take away or limit financial freedom. Are you content with your financial abundance or are you choosing to live the life of victimhood and discontent with your financial situation?

When did wanting abundance and financial freedom become an evil, greedy, self-consuming goal? I believe that this ideal may have partially been created as a defensive coping mechanism for those in the lower and middle classes who did not feel that they could achieve an abundant lifestyle, but we all deserve a life of abundance. It may have also stemmed from those corrupt, high-powered entities who wanted us to feel inferior and unworthy of obtaining our own personal version of financial abundance. With this false belief, they are trying to take away your power. Don't let them.

What value do you place on yourself? Is it the value that was given to you as a child or told to you as a young adult? Do you realize that you are in control of this answer? What are you manifesting into your life right now? Is it minimal, obvious achievements, or do you mentally, emotionally, and spiritually reach higher? You can achieve so much more than you think! One of my favorite quotes about this is from Winnie-the-Pooh: "Promise me you'll always remember: You're braver than you believe, and stronger than you seem, and smarter than you think."[22] Thank you, sweet Christopher Robbin, for reminding us all of this simple truth. Do you realize, around the time that I wrote this book, that about 68% of the

---

[22] Promise me you'll always remember: You're braver than you believe, and stronger than you seem, and smarter than you think. A. A. Milne - philosiblog

world's richest people are 'self-made'? We all start the same way, yet our mindsets, ambition, determination, and perseverance set us apart. Think about that: our strong desire to achieve something typically requires only determination, hard work, and energy; this is our strength. Our vitality is required to sustain the physical and mental activities needed to achieve those ambitious goals. Truly, this is the starting point in achieving this type of success. This is a reality that we need to wrap our brains around. We hold the keys to our own success. In fact, not only can you achieve financial abundance, but imagine what you could do with that type of wealth for our world. If you had that type of money, what would you do with it? I think about this often, as I am sure many people do. Of course, most people's first response is narcissistic, serving a selfish purpose like buying a bigger house, car, boats, a yacht, a plane, or vacation homes. But after all that, then what? What would you do? How would you want to impact the world to make it a better, safer and healthier place? Would you start up a foundation to help third-world countries? Would you help inner-city youth? How would you leave your footprint on this world? I would hope and pray that each of us would share our financial blessings with others who are less fortunate. When I refer to those less fortunate, I am not talking about the takers of the world, those who chose to be victims and do absolutely nothing to better their situations. I am talking about the innocents of the world, those who had no choice or say in their dire situations. Those are the people I want to assist, if they want my support—those who are willing to reach their hands up to mine to be pulled up into a better situation that would provide them with opportunities to live a better life, their authentic life. We all desire better things in life, but one thing I know for sure is that when you focus on the needs of others, without effort, your own needs seem to be fulfilled. Give grace, and grace will be given to you. It's such a beautiful concept yet so quickly overlooked and forgotten by our competitive, selfish, and money-hungry society. Just think about it. What gifts do you have, and who can you share them with? When you learn to share your gifts, you will receive more gifts to give. It is such a beautiful truth! Do not be afraid to give without expectations; you will get back more than you know. Sometimes our financial blessings come to us wearing many different masks—no pun intended, COVID!

It all starts with gratitude for what you have in this very moment. What are you grateful for? Make a list of one, two, or three things each day that you are heartily grateful for—those things that make your heart squeeze and bring tears to your eyes. Whether you choose a simple or extravagant life, this is the starting point in living a financially abundant lifestyle.

PART 4
Your Thoughts

Illustrated by Grant S. Morrison

CHAPTER 22

Your Thoughts Shape Your Life

The saying "What you think about, you bring about" is true. Our thoughts can be positive or negative, helpful or harmful, self-rewarding or self-sabotaging. Have you ever tried to go through one day with only positive thoughts? If you have then you know how insanely hard it is. The behavior chain links each situation to a thought, which produces feelings. Those feelings lead to an action, and those actions are followed by consequences. Based on our thoughts, those actions may result in good or bad consequences. I believe that it is our feelings that are the driving force of our thoughts. We humans experience so many different feelings, and they can be categorized into two separate groups: positive and negative. What are you going to focus on in your own life? You can focus on the lower dense energies of your ego, which is your false, shell-self. Your false self wants you to believe in untruths that result in feelings of judgment, separation, anger, jealousy, resentment, fear, indifference, self-importance, self-denial, disgust, loss, pride, complaining, materialism, and basically being someone you really aren't. When you focus on that part of your ego, you will bring about this darkness, the shadow self, which we all have. If that option does not sound appealing to you, you can focus on your higher soul, which is your true self. Your true self wants you to believe in the truths of who you really are, which result in the feelings of acceptance, oneness, compassion, security, joy, happiness, forgiveness, equality, peace, wisdom, self-acceptance, spiritualism, empathy, and so many more positive things that grow from one simple word, *love*. Once you learn the truth, you cannot go back. You learn how to illuminate your shadow side, and with that insight, your spiritual, true, authentic soul self will flourish. Don't get me wrong—I feel that, living in our human bodies, we do need the shell of our ego-selves to protect us in certain moments of life, but we cannot allow them to dictate our souls' purposes.

When we become more mindful of our thoughts, we begin to understand the power within ourselves. With this knowledge, we discover the ability to manage our own minds. A managed mind creates a peaceful, happy, and fulfilling life. Happiness is not achieved by the pursuit of happiness but rather by living the right way. How do you live the right way? Well, only you can answer that for yourself. For me, the right way involves living a life of integrity, which is the quality of being honest and having strong moral principles and moral uprightness. Living with integrity is achieved through productive and positive daily actions and choices.

When we choose to live a spiritually, socially, emotionally, mentally, physically, occupationally, environmentally, and financially balanced lifestyle with a mindset of integrity, we have chosen to be the best version of ourselves. It is only then that we achieve the fulfillment of living life as our authentic selves. When we discover our authentic selves, we have the opportunity and ability to share the positive consequences of living our authentic lives with the world, which in turn can add value to other people's lives. "Be careful how you think; your life is shaped by your thoughts." (Proverbs 4:23 Good News Translation, or GNT).

> "The greater danger for most of us lies not in setting our aim too high and falling short; but in setting our aim too low, and achieving our mark."[23] —Michelangelo Buonarroti

---

[23] Di Ladvico Bunarroti Simoni, Michelangelo. "Area of Design." https:/areaofdesign. com. 1962

CHAPTER 23

Protect Your Power

D o not confuse your own worth and value by taking your self-perception from others. You are no less than any other person on this earth. When you find yourself feeling hurt, defeated, unloved, and unappreciated, you are giving others your power and not living your authentic life.

There will be times in life when you feel like you are the pitcher of water filling up everyone else's cups, yet you feel that you cannot find anywhere to refill your pitcher. When you find yourself in this situation, remind yourself of two things: 1) find your water fountain, your tribe, the people in your life who fill you up, including yourself, self-love; and 2) learn to protect yourself from energy takers, the people who want to suck you dry. You may have to learn to love from a distance. Do not feel guilty about this. You cannot give what you do not already possess.

When you do not know who you truly are, you will find yourself accepting less than you truly deserve. You may feel like a doormat to others. It's a difficult paradox to be in because, on one hand, you are a caring, loving, giving soul and you want to shine your light on others, yet when you do, certain people take advantage of you and try to either suck up your light or throw their shadows over your light. This is because you have allowed their beliefs of who you are to distort your own self-worth. Find the true you, and you will find the life worthy of you and nothing less than your greatness. Love yourself enough to recognize toxic relationships and learn to love from a distance and walk away.

How do you learn to protect your power? There are many ways you can learn this, including meditation, Reiki, and prayer.

CHAPTER 24

Finding Peace and Realigning to Your Authentic Self:

Self-Love and Acceptance

What is your mantra, your goals that you are working on right now? What are you manifesting in your life? Who is the real you, and do you love who you are?

I believe that the wholeness of a person is made up of two parts: the spiritual self, which is our true self, and the ego self, which I think of as a protective force field wrapped around our true self.

It can be challenging and difficult to uncover the authentic self because our egos always seem to get in our way. When we allow the ego to get in the way, we beat ourselves up about past mistakes. We become critical of who we are. We become our own worst enemies, which can lead to self-sabotage. The more we feed our ego-selves, the stronger they will grow. We find ourselves living in a state of fear, anger, resentment, jealousy, and self-doubt.

If you are searching for the authentic, real you, you will uncover and discover all the gifts you have and realize that your spirit is love—love for yourself and love for the world. Without the connection to your soul, your spiritual and authentic self, you cannot share the full potential of your spiritual gifts to the world. And isn't that what we all want? Aren't we all seeking our true purpose here on earth? How do you find your authentic self? Your mental body (ego) wants to talk over your spiritual body (soul self).

Below are some tools that I have used in my life to connect with my spiritual self:

1. Meditation – Yes, I said the "M" word. Listen, I did not even start meditating until I turned fifty. I am not sure if I was a little intimidated by the unknown or if I was just too darn busy to find five minutes to take some time for myself. Meditation is a time of falling into yourself. It is a time to find peace with the amazingness of yourself. The first few times I meditated, I used a voice-guided recording, which I found to be helpful. I started terribly slow, and gradually over time I've increased my meditating time, which has afforded me a deeper meditation state of mind. It is refreshing, recharging, enlightening, and so very peaceful. Thank you to one of the coolest meditation coaches I have had, Holly Smith. Meditation is about finding your zero point and finding cohesion within yourself. It's about slowing down your mental mind and grounding into your spiritual body. Meditation involves listening.

2. Prayer – I have separated meditation and prayer, but for some people they are one and the same. For me, they are two separate activities. When I reflect upon prayer, the first face that comes into my mind is that of my father-in-law, Jerry Fryer, a.k.a. The Reece. He is the type of man who begins each morning in solitude with his Bible. He is a man of unwavering faith and love. I call him the rock of the Fryer legacy. There are so many ways that we can pray, and I really do not feel that there is a wrong way or that one way is better than another. Prayer is a very personal thing, and you need to take the time to figure out what works best for you. Going to church and praying with your congregation is helpful, and reading the Bible is another great way to pray. It's called the living word because, no matter how many times you read the same passage,

you will get something different out of it based on where you are in your life. I read the Bible nearly every day. I read just one passage, and I carry my interpretation of its meaning with me throughout the day. Sometimes I receive multiple signs throughout the day that confirm and align with my reading, but sometimes I do not and that is OK. God speaks to us through prayer, the living word (Bible), other believers, and circumstances. Starting your day with a reading opens your heart and mind to the whispers of God, which you might miss if you do not start the day off right. Prayer might mean just being with other believers whether in a Bible study group, at a church gathering, or just with friends, family, and neighbors. If you try one way and it does not work, please do not give up. You will need to figure out what works best for you. I bet that if you say a prayer, God will provide you with an answer. Also, do not forget about all our amazing archangels and saints! I also pray to them nearly every day. I say the "Saint Anthony, Saint Anthony, something is lost that must be found" prayer every day—and I mean *every day*! And you know what? He never fails me because I always find what I am looking for. I'll talk more about archangels later. Spiritual meditation, as mentioned above, offers similar results, but I feel that prayer involves more "talking" and meditation involves more "listening." Pray for the highest good of yourself, others and the universe.

3. Chakra clearing and cleansing – These words might scare or intimidate some people, but this works. You might want to start with a trained chakra healer first, but you can also learn to clear and realign your own chakras. It's an attunement of alignment of your spiritual, physical, emotional, mental and physical self. It starts with you and aligning with the higher power, God, I am, source, or whatever you resonate with, coupled with grounding into Gaia Earth.

4. Reiki – This word may resonate with you or seem foreign and a bit frightening. Reiki originated in Japan with a theology teacher, Mikao Usui. The symbols are of Sanskrit origin. It is a Japanese method that activates the relaxation response at a very deep level. It promotes rebalancing by creating an environment for the body

and mind to begin to heal themselves through the flow of energy. While writing this book, I became a Reiki-Certified Master. I use crystals in my energy healing sessions, because that's what resonates with me. I also channel guardian angels and archangels when I perform my sessions. I find fulfillment working with my clients, assisting them in clearing and realigning themselves. I am not a healer, but I am a vessel or channel of the healing energies from source, God, as well as Gaia Earth. It is similar to chakra clearing, but there is a difference. Reiki channels energy in a specific pattern to restore balance and promotes healing. Reiki differs as the person needing healing draws the needed energy from the channel of a Reiki professional through the laying of the hands to increase the universal life force energy. It promotes relaxation, detoxification of the bodies systems, destroys energy blocks, and provides a new life-force vitality. It will also increase the frequency of vibrations of the body.

5. Find your tribe – Once you begin to clear and heal yourself from within, you need to look outside yourself and ask, "Who is on your spiritual team?" For me, it is God, Jesus, the Holy Spirit, my guardian angels, the archangels, my parents, my husband, my children, my extended family, and my forever sisters, who really are my spiritual tribe. I have found that the more I uncover my true authentic spiritual self, the more I attract people in my life who are like-minded. This is a crucial and key part of this process because we all want and physically need to be wanted and accepted by others. When you go through your own spiritual journey and awakening, you might find yourself feeling alone, like an outsider. This can feel scary, but when you have others around you who are also on their own spiritual journeys, there is a common thread. This is comforting because not only does someone else understand the transformation that you are going through, but together, you can grow and transcend at a faster rate and higher frequency, which can be pretty amazing. Surround yourself with people who support you and your dreams. This transformation is without judgment but shared with a divine love.

6. Where is your special spot — the place to which you can physically or mentally escape for moments of deep thought, meditation, yoga, and prayer? I envision a beach, sandy white, almost glistening in the sunlight with aqua blue and turquoise waves pounding into the shore. I hear the waves rippling in, one after another, almost like an assault, but the sound is peaceful to my heart and soul. Since I live in Michigan, I cannot physically get to this location, but my new home has an amazing backyard oasis with a beautiful built-in pool and gardens. I use my peaceful backyard as my special spot to connect. I also felt this connection when I was in Sedona, Arizona, facing my fear of heights, after climbing a mountain to watch a magnificent sunrise. In that moment I felt one with God.

7. Self-love and acceptance —You cannot heal the body until you heal the mind. You cannot heal the mind without self-love. You need to learn to let go and accept yourself for who you are. I'm not saying that you should stop improving yourself; you should never stop learning and growing. But what I am saying is love who you are right now in this very moment and in each moment to follow. We all make mistakes, but it is applying the lessons from those mistakes that helps us reach our full potential. It starts with love.

CHAPTER 25

Understanding the Chakra System

The chakra system is traceable to one of the most authoritative Hindu texts, the Vedas,[24] from the second millennium BCE, and is present in Tantric Buddhism as well. Chakras are both internal and external. We all have chakra points within our bodies, as does the earth. Earth chakras are remarkably similar to energy vortexes, like the trip I formally mentioned I took to Sedona, Arizona. It was honestly one of the most spiritual and rewarding journeys I have ever taken. I felt and physically saw the positive spiritual energies there. I would highly suggest that each of you take a trip to Sedona. I was brought to my knees with spiritual gratitude multiple times on my five-day trip. As for the chakra system, think of it as a two-lane highway: heading south, you purge the negative, and heading north, you recharge the positive.

In the United States, the root chakra is believed to be located at Mount Shasta, California. The sacral chakra is believed to be at Lake Titicaca, the home to Isla del Sol, or the Island of the Sun, a Bolivian island at the Peruvian-Bolivian border. The solar plexus chakra is said to be located at the Tjuta Rock Formations, Uluru and Kata Tjuta, which are eighteen miles apart in the Australian desert. The heart chakra is believed to be in two towns in Southern England, Shaftesbury and Glastonbury, that are thirty miles apart and is believed to include Stonehenge. The throat chakra

---

24 Debroy, Bibek and Dipavali. "The Holy Vedas." 1994.

115

is a perfect right triangle believed to have corners at the Great Pyramid in Egypt, at Mount Sinai, and at Jerusalem's Mount of Olives. The third-eye chakra is currently believed to be located in Glastonbury, England, but this is the only chakra that can shift locations due to the axis rotation of the earth. The crown chakra is believed to be located at Mount Kailash in the Himalayas of Tibet. God created all of this and wants me to share it with you.

Following are the characteristics of each of the chakras.

Earth Chakra

- Color: brown
- Suggested stone: hematite, garnet, tourmaline
- Essential oils: white fir, black spruce, ylang, pine
- Connects you to the earth
- Right: to connect
- Positive qualities: stability, reliability, and thoughtfulness
- Affirmation: I am stable, grounded, and deeply rooted into Gaia Earth. I feel safe and secure and trust myself. I make healthy choices.

Root Chakra

- Color: red
- Suggested crystal: red jasper
- Essential oils: patchouli, sandalwood
- Encourages grounding and balance, self-esteem, and confidence
- Protects against negative energies
- Right: to have
- Positive qualities: stability, vitality, loyalty, prosperity, patience, tenacity, career success
- Malfunction: bowel, blood or bone disorders, obesity, anorexia, anxiety, spaciness, financial problems, chronic fear, materialism, instability
- Affirmations: I am grounded, safe, and secure. I make a good living doing what I love. I am stable, strong, and healthy.

Sacral Chakra

- Color: orange
- Suggested crystal: carnelian, moonstone
- Essential oils: jasmine, geranium, orange blossom
- Stimulates the imagination, releases negativity and limiting beliefs
- Inspires passion and creativity
- Right: to feel
- Positive qualities: joy, creativity, adaptability, sensuality, fertility, pleasure, sexuality
- Malfunction: Genital issues, sexual or fertility problems, rigidity, isolation, hip or sacroiliac joint problems, dehydration
- Affirmations: I am creative and adaptable. I am a sensual and sexual being. I can enjoy the pleasures of life.

Solar Plexus Chakra

- Color: yellow
- Suggested crystals: topaz, citrine, tiger's eye
- Essential oils: basil, ginger, bergamot
- Inspires integrity and the correct use of power
- Assist in achieving goals and recognizing inner strengths
- Right: to act
- Positive qualities: power, confidence, charisma, strong will, humor, leadership, mental clarity
- Malfunction: digestive issues, kidney or liver problems, timidity, rage, diabetes, ulcers, domination, chronic fatigue, low self-esteem
- Affirmations: I can do anything I set my mind to. I am powerful and use power wisely. I have a good sense of humor and laugh often.

Heart Chakra

- Color: green (also pink)
- Suggested crystals: pink quartz, emerald, jade
- Essential oils: rose, benzoin, eucalyptus

- Promotes love and compassion; stimulates emotional intelligence, healing, and an opening of the heart
- Right: to love
- Positive qualities: love, trust, healing, equanimity, compassion, connection, surrender
- Malfunction: asthma, apnea, heart or lung problems, breast cancer, allergies, immune disorders, loneliness, antisocial behavior, thymus issues
- Affirmations: I am loving and lovable. I am deeply compassionate. I am a source of healing in the world.

Throat Chakra

- Color: light blue
- Suggested crystals: sodalite, celestite, turquoise, lapis lazuli
- Essential oils: hyssop, clementine, blue chamomile
- Inspires clear communication and freedom of expression; dissolves old patterns of repression and judgement
- Right: to express
- Positive qualities: truth, purpose, expression, artistry, service, synchronicity, communication
- Malfunction: thyroid or hearing problems, teeth or gum issues, lying, tonsils, stiff neck or shoulders, TMJ, lack of purpose, fear of speaking
- Affirmations: I know my truth and I share it. I am guided by my deepest purpose. My life is guided by divine synchronicity.

Third-Eye Chakra

- Color: deep blue/indigo
- Suggested crystals: opal, lapis lazuli, azurite, amethyst
- Essential oils: rosemary, sage, ylang
- Opens the third eye, stimulates intuition, facilitates inner knowing, stimulates the mind and brings clarity
- Right: to perceive

- Positive qualities: vision, intuition, dreams, insight, perception, clairvoyance, equanimity
- Malfunction: vision problems, migraines, nightmares, bipolar disorder, sleep disorders, sinus issues, hallucinations, lack of intuition
- Affirmations: I am intuitive and follow my inner guidance. I always see the big picture. I avidly follow my dreams.

Crown Chakra

- Color: amethyst purple
- Suggested crystals: clear quartz, amethyst, diamond
- Essential oils: myrrh, violet, frankincense
- Aids connection to the divine and heightens consciousness
- Enhances meditation and prayer
- Right: to know
- Positive qualities: unity, wisdom, awareness, intelligence, understanding, miracles, bliss
- Malfunction: Alzheimer's, confusion, spaciness, mental illness, over intellectualism, depression, apathy, learning disabilities
- Affirmations: I am intelligent and aware. I am one with everything. I have endless, great ideas.

Star Chakra

- Color: white or white gold
- Suggested crystals: clear quartz, diamond
- Essential oils: rose, patchouli, myrrh, lavender
- Described as the seat of the soul and is the direct connection of your higher self, the Akashic records, your karmic past, and your past lives.
- Located in your etheric body, six inches above your head within your auric field
- Carries all the information for your soul's past and present purpose for being here
- Right: to fulfill your soul's purpose

- Positive qualities: acts as a chakra balancing tool, direct link to all information regarding your Akashic records, understanding your current lifetime fears and challenges and how to overcome them, increases psychic abilities
- Malfunction: may cause feelings of being upset, uneasiness, and shock
- Affirmations: I am divine light. I am divine love.

Author Jeddah Mali wrote, "Your body is full of energy, your emotions are harmonious and warm, your thoughts are bright and clear, your heart is open and loving, you are kind, compassionate and understanding, you communicate clearly and cleanly, you are able to see your inner being, and you are able to know the truth of who you really are. Simply use intention to allow the maximum flow possible."[25]

Schedule a session with a local certified Reiki healer or Reiki crystal healer. You can also visit my website, www.mindfulblissliving.com, for additional information on booking a Reiki individual or group session, a motivational life coach session, an individual or group meditation session, or an individual or group angel message session.

---

[25] Mali, Jeddah. www.Intelligent.life

CHAPTER 26

Aligning Your Chakras: Self-Technique

Recognize your flow of energy—your PEF, or personal flow of energy—via opening your chakra energy levels. Your body craves balance and homeostasis, spiritually, mentally, and physically. There are many chakra-alignment meditation exercises online, and you need to try them all out until you find the one that resonates with you. It might seem uncomfortable or weird, and that is OK. There are many other options on the internet or an in-person session. We have nine primary energy systems that are backed by electromagnetic measurements and acknowledged and understood by every culture in our world. Donna Eden described the nine energy systems that impact the body as follows: meridians, chakras, aura, basic grid, Celtic weave, five rhythms, triple warmer, radiant circuits, and the electrics.[26]

---

[26] Eden, Donna "Nine energy systems"

CHAPTER 27

I Am Grateful for This Moment: Living in the Now

You cannot live fully in the present moment when you are hanging onto the past. Your past regrets, mistakes, struggles, fears, and disappointments can be the barrier that is keeping you from fully embracing the present and receiving all the gifts it can bring. The past teaches us life lessons, the future holds our hopes and dreams, but the present is where the action happens. Remember that a sinner has a future and a saint had a past. Be in the moment. Be fully aware of all things. Sometimes—let's be honest, most times in life, we are in autopilot. We live in our daily doldrums, and we miss some of life's most cherished and free blessings. Try to not be distracted by past mistakes and life regrets. Equally, do not get caught up on future tasks, agendas, plans, and responsibilities. Just live in the moment. I realize that this is so much harder than it sounds. It is tough. If you choose to live life on autopilot, you will miss out on so much. You might be missing what your true mission and soul purpose is within this lifetime. Don't you sometimes think, *Wait. Is this really it? Is this what I am supposed to be doing? Is this my mission and purpose?* Be mindfully aware of the signs that the universe is sending you daily. Be aware of the people who are weaved into your life for a day, a week, a month, a year, a decade, or a lifetime. These people, situations, and circumstances are placed on your path for a reason. They are in your life to teach you a lesson, to learn a lesson from you, or possibly to assist you both in advancing to the next level of spiritual awareness. Some souls are lifers, and these special souls are part of our collective soul families. Our paths are meant to cross because our journeys are meant to be shared. Live life at a higher frequency and altitude. When you do, you will be able to see the big picture of how we are all connected as if from the view of an eagle. It's hard to have an eagle's view if you are still clinging to the boulders that keep you stagnant and weighing you down. In order to grow, you have to flow. In order to flow, you have to let go of the boulders that are anchoring you down. Untether and elevate.

CHAPTER 28

Finding Your Destiny

First find what ignites and stirs your soul. In that truth, you will find your destiny. God places those passions inside each of us for a reason. He knows that if the desire is strong enough, it will motivate most of us into action that will lead to change and growth, which ultimately leads us on the beautiful journey to our soul destiny. It is the journey that refines us, educates us, and strengthens us, and in that process, we find our destiny. Sometimes it feels like we are meandering like water down a steep mountain that turns into a stream and zigzags down, gently rolling with what appears to be no thought given to its pattern, yet it gathers and carries rocks and gravel down with its current. The zigs and zags take us to different places as well, providing opportunities to meet new people and experience new places and things that we never imagined. The rocks and gravel we carry with us are our experiences, our wisdom, our strengths, and our heartaches, which lead us to our destination at the bottom of the mountain—our sole purpose, which is our soul's purpose.

Honestly, it is really a simple answer: finding your destiny lies in finding your authentic self. Once you find your authentic self, love it. Love it with all your might. Love yourself as you love a child, maybe your own child, or if you do not have children, love the child within your soul. You may be quirky, weird, free-spirited, fun-loving, faith-filled, intense, social, antisocial—whatever you are, love it.

CHAPTER 29

A Mind in Opposition

The mind cannot occupy two opposing thoughts at the same time. Faith and fear cannot occupy the same space. As I mentioned earlier, the acronym for *fear* is "false evidence appearing real." What are you letting occupy your mind? Believe me, I understand this struggle because I too have succumbed to negative thoughts occupying my mind. Sometimes, the fear was so intense that I allowed it to consume me. I became addicted to the negative. Since deepening my awareness of the lie that fear brings, I have learned to stop myself from falling prey to the fear. Instead, I realign and regroup. In these moments of weakness, you need to find strength in your foundation of faith and grace. Faith is the strong belief of a higher power, based on spiritual apprehension rather than proof. Grace teaches us to let go and let God happen. The biblical principle for this is, "My grace is sufficient for you, for my power is made perfect in weakness" (2 Corinthians 12:9).

In those moments when fear sneaks into your heart and mind, you first need awareness to realize what is happening. After the realization process, you must remove the negative pull that surrounds you on a mental, physical, and spiritual level. Fill that void with love—the love that God or your higher power has for you on a spiritual level and the love of self. It is also helpful to receive support on the physical level through your tribe. The people who believe in you, fill your cup, and make you feel loved, appreciated, and powerful are your tribe, and they help you stay the course as you continue on your soul journey. Satan is like a thief in the night. He sneaks in like a slow-festering cancer. You do not see it, feel it, hear it, smell it, or taste it, yet he wreaks havoc on your mind. Do not let him win. You know the end of the story: God or your higher power has the *glory*! Find your strength in that truth.

I have Ephesians 6:10–18, the verses about the armor of God, posted in my drawer at work. When things get tough, I open my drawer and read it aloud: "Finally, be strong in the Lord and in his mighty power. Put on the full armor of God so that you can take your stand against the devil's schemes. For our struggles are not against flesh and blood, but against the rulers, against the authorities, against the powers of the dark world and against the spiritual forces of evil in the heavenly realms. Therefore, put on the full armor of God, so that when the day of evil comes, you may be able to stand your ground, and after you have done everything, to stand. Stand firm then, with the belt of truth buckled around your waist, with the breastplate of righteousness in place, and with your feet fitted with the readiness that comes from the gospel of peace. In addition to all this, take up the shield of faith, with which salvation and the sword of the spirit, which is the word of God. And pray in the Spirit on all occasions with all kinds of prayers and requests. With this in mind, be alert and always keep on praying for all the saints" (Ephesians 6:10–18).

Basically, you need to make a daily decision to be victorious in all your endeavors of righteousness. Tell yourself that you will conquer, and you will be victorious. The mind, coupled with faith, can be a powerful thing. Believe me, there will be people in your life, on social media, and in the "fake news," as well as ancestral untruths, that want to rob you of your existence, your energy, your being, your faith, your joy, your life, and your journey's ultimate destination, but you have the power to say, "Nope, not today." Stand up for yourself, walk away from the fear, and do not let them win. One of my favorite biblical quotes is, "Get behind me, Satan! You are a stumbling block to me; you do not have in mind the things of God, but the things of men" (Matthew 16:23).

Do not get me wrong—even though I have written this book, I too am still a work in progress. I continue to run toward my goal line, learning life's lessons along the way and tweaking my dreams and goals as I discover the meaning of my own existence. Choose what occupies your mind by allowing the positive to flow and release the negative.

William Ward once wrote, "A pessimist complains about the wind; the optimist expects it to change; the realist adjusts his sails."[27]

---

[27] Ward, William. "Fountains of Faith." Droke House Addition. 1970

CHAPTER 30

Change

Change is freaking awesome! Embrace change, despite the fear that comes with it. Squeeze it like you squeeze lemons when you are making homemade lemonade. What is change? Change involves something to alter or transform into a different course or direction. The shift includes modifications resulting in a new outcome or result. Yes, it takes movement mentally, physically, and spiritually. It can be exhilarating, exhausting, and scary as hell, but do it anyway! Change is moving forward. It is the flow of energy, and nothing good comes without energy and change. Change is required for transformation. Without transformation, you remain stagnant in the murky waters of the soul. Embrace the changes in life. Change allows new people, places, and opportunities to enter your path required for your journey toward your own personal finish line.

Sometimes change is a voluntary choice, but other times it is forced upon us by other people or situations. When it is voluntary, it is easier to adjust your sails to the shifting winds because it was your initial choice, but when it is involuntary, it can lead to feelings of fear, anxiety, anger, and resentment. Those are lower based ego emotions and reactions. When you feel them, acknowledge them and move on. Ask yourself, *What am I supposed to learn at this moment? Where's the silver lining in the clouds? Where is the rainbow and the pot of gold?* When you choose to look at change as a positive rather than a negative, you will receive positive results. Do not ever be afraid of change, because it is needed to get you to the next level of life.

CHAPTER 31

Living Your Dream Life

Strive to live your life genuinely and authentically in each realm of existence, achieving and implementing the eight dimensions of wellness: social, spiritual, emotional, environmental, occupational, intellectual, physical, and financial. For me, the key to my self-discovery and growth is to become the best version of myself and to be this best self in all aspects of my life. I want to be genuine, authentic, and loving in all that I do. Do I succeed all the time? No, but I give it my best effort, and when I do slip, I catch myself faster than I did in my past, which helps me to get back on the right track of my life.

We all want to feel loved, valued, appreciated, needed, and important. You are near the top of your mountain. Are you ready to see the amazing view that God has in store for you? Can you anticipate that moment when you can breathe in the fresh air at your mountaintop and feel that sense of freedom that comes in those moments of feeling that you have arrived? When you place your focus on the betterment of yourself, you in turn better those around you. Fix yourself, and you help others fix themselves. Take time to internalize these thoughts about who you want to be and live a balanced life socially, spiritually, emotionally, environmentally, occupationally, intellectually, physically, and financially. It is different for each person. It is our perspective, our lives, our choices, and ultimately our destinations.

PART 5

Heaven

Photographed by Jennifer Tobias

CHAPTER 32

What Does Heaven Look Like?

What do you think heaven looks like? We have heard so many stories from people who have had near-death experiences and have shared their visions of the world beyond. We have seen numerous sketched and painted images of the beautiful, green, luscious gardens and streets of gold with angels dressed in white robes. You may have read the Bible and other ancient writings depicting what heaven looks like. As for me—and I know it's going to sound a bit crazy—I envision heaven as I walk up to the pearly gates a little bit like when I'm in my spinning class or a Butts, Guts and Guns class and I hear my instructor change to the cool-down music, at which point I become giddy with excitement because I know that I did it. I ran the race and made it to the finish line, even if it's only a one-hour workout class. That feeling is awesome. I think that when I reach heaven, it might feel a little like that. "I have fought the good fight, I have finished the race, I have kept the faith" (2 Timothy 4:7). I also reflect on my travels to the Caribbean and to Sedona, when I felt the love of God wrap around me so tightly in His loving arms that it brought me to tears in my prayers of gratitude.

I also reflect on the book *Prayer of Jabez: Breaking through to the Blessed Life*,[28] written by Bruce Wilkinson. It is an extraordinary story of how,

---

[28] Bruce Wilkinson. "Mr. Jones Goes to Heaven." p.24. *The Prayer of Jabez, Breaking Through the Blessed Life*. Sisters, Oregon: Multnomah Publishing Company. 1984

when we just ask for help and intercession from God, we all can receive divine favor, anointing, and protection. You can find the story of Jabez in the Bible, but if you do not know where to look you just might miss it. "Oh, that You would bless me indeed, and enlarge my territory, that Your hand be with me, and that You would keep me from evil, that I may not cause pain!" (1 Chronicles 4:10). One of my favorite stories in Wilkinson's book is the one about Mr. Jones. Mr. Jones makes it to heaven, where he is met by Peter and gained entrance. Peter takes Mr. Jones on a tour of heaven, during which Mr. Jones notices an enormous white building in the distance and asks about it. Peter tells him that he would not want to see what is inside. This makes Mr. Jones very curious, and eventually, at the end of his tour, he is allowed access into the building. He is astonished at what he sees—endless rows of beautifully wrapped gifts with crimson red bows. He notices that there are names on each of the boxes and wonders if he too has a gift. Peter tells him that there is indeed a box for him, so Mr. Jones eagerly searches for it. Once he finds it, he pops off the lid and releases a big sigh. You see, the box contains all the blessings that God had wanted to give Mr. Jones while on earth but could not because Mr. Jones never asked God for those blessings.

"You do not have because you do not ask God. When you ask, you do not receive because you ask with wrong motives that you may spend what you get on your pleasures" (James 4:2b–3).

When you ask with the right intentions, you shall receive. Be ready and open to receive the gifts that will be granted to you. Take those gifts and multiply them to share with others.

CHAPTER 33

The Living Word, Numbers, and Their Biblical Meaning

I am including some biblical and numerological meaning of numbers because I have always been fascinated with the unknown. Maybe it's the Scorpio in me, but since I was a small girl, I have been intrigued by the mysteries of the world, the things hidden in the undercurrent of life. I love discovering how things are connected at a high level, including energy, numbers, patterns, and coincidences versus fate of the universe. I am compelled to learn more about these topics because I feel that, through this knowledge and understanding, we can propel ourselves to a higher level of love and find the simple joys of living. So if you did not have this information before, you do now.

- 1 = The number 1 is divisible only by itself. It is independence, unity between God the Father and Jesus, and a new beginning or a new cycle, like a snake shedding the old skin to reveal the new skin. When you see the numbers 1, 11, 111 or 11:11, you are being asked to be more conscious of your energetic awareness because this is a time of manifestation, so stay positive and manifest your dreams. The number 11:11 is the most common sequence seen around the world. It is a powerful sign of spiritual awakening and ascension.

- 2 = Union, division, or verification of facts by witnesses; also, the connection between husband and wife and between Jesus and the church. This number is about balance, duality, intuition, and connection. It is a sign bringing your awareness to cooperate with others and work on relationships within your life. It is also a healing number and is known for intuition and psychic development. The number 22 is a master number that enhances harmony, intuition, and the energy of the original number 2.
- 3 = Completeness (to a lesser degree than 7); divine completeness and perfection. It represents the Trinity. The number 3 is all about creativity and speaking the truth. It is also about community and being social. When you see 33 or 333, it is a message from your angels that you are on the right track and it is time to share your gifts with the world.
- 4 = Creation, world. It is a solid number, with four pillars of support that ground you and afford stability. It is about working hard and having your foundations in place. It is also associated with honesty and integrity. The number 44 is also a master number and amplifies the number 4, which is about organization, practicality, and balance. Think north, south, east, and west and summer, fall, winter, and spring.
- 5 = God's grace, goodness, and favor toward humankind; grace. It also signifies changes, challenges, and conflicts. Change does not need to be scary because growth cannot happen without change. When you see 5, 55, or 555, it encourages you to be free and experience new adventures, which can lead to spiritual awakening. When your vibrations rise, your surroundings, including people, places, and employment, may also change. Lower vibrational people, places, and patterns are no longer serving you.
- 6 = Human weakness, the evils of Satan, and the manifestation of sin. Some believe that the number 6 represents harmonious, loving, and nurturing characteristics, associated with love and family. It can also be linked to a woman bearing a child, the womb of a mother. Fertility. It is about family or mending relationships, including self-love. The number 6 is also linked to and interpreted

with your learning or receiving holistic medication modalities, like Reiki and crystal energy healing.

- 7 = The foundation of God's Word represents completeness and perfection (both physical and spiritual), resurrection, spiritual completion. The number 7 is connected to introverts and to those connected on a higher spiritual plane. The number 7 is also linked to yoga, meditation, and spiritual or metaphysical studies. The numbers 77 and 777 are highly expressive and creative and are urging you to investigate the geometric, kabbalah, or other ancient sources of wisdom and guidance. These numbers are telling you to learn, teach, create, and inspire others.

- 8 = New beginnings, new order, born again, balance. The number 8 is also intricately linked to the Chinese and Hong Kong beliefs of abundance and prosperity. The numbers 8, 88, and 888 are incredibly lucky numbers and bring a flow of financial blessings into your life. The number 8 is associated with your career, but you must rise above your ego and pull into your oversoul through alignment to your life purpose so that you do not fall into self-sabotage. When you see 88 or 888, this is an incredibly special message from your angels that you are about to experience abundance in your life. Their message is like the saying, "What you think about, you bring about." Flip an 8 on its side and it becomes the infinity sign.

- 9 = Symbolizes divine completeness or conveys the meaning of finality, divine completeness from the Father, fruit of the Spirit. The number 9 is a sign of reaching completion. It is also a message for you to let go of what no longer serves you, which includes people, places, situations, and employment. The number 9 represents selflessness, compassion, and humanitarian characteristics, like charities and volunteer work. The numbers 9, 99 and 999 signify spiritual awakening and ascension. It is about letting go and seeking closure so you can move on to better things.

- 10 = Also viewed as a complete and perfect number; signifies testimony, law, responsibility, and the completeness of order.

- 11 = Symbolizes disorder, chaos, and judgment. This number is also a master number (see number 1). It also reveals enlightenment, evolution, achievement, and discovery.
- 12 = Considered a perfect number of symbolizing God's power and authority; also symbolizes completeness or the nation of Israel as a whole, government perfection. This number 12 is 1 + 2 = 3, the Holy Trinity.
- 13 = Symbolic for rebellion, lawlessness, apostasy, and depravity but also reduces to the number 4; and is also connected to the feminine of fertility, love, peace, and light. It is truly a positive number that has been used by those who want control as a negative number. Together, 1 + 3 = 4, which means balance, foundation, north, south, east, west. Don't be blinded by the flashing lights; look behind the veil, the number 13 is a very strong symbolism and has great power.

CHAPTER 34

Angels Are Real!

Since I was a little girl, I have been drawn to angels. I have been intrigued by them for as long as I can remember. After the deaths of family members, at a young age, I channeled angels. Passed-on loved ones would visit me and give me messages. Instead of being fearful, I embraced this gift and nurtured it. The older I get, the more I find myself yearning to build a more intimate relationship with each of our angels. Angels hold a unique, majestic power under our creator, God. I was first drawn to archangel Raphael, most likely because he was the archangel of the Catholic church I attended when I was a little girl. After growing up, I moved and began attending a new church, St. Michael, which led to my interest in archangel Michael. I memorized the St. Michael prayer and said it not only every week after our church service, but every morning as I walked out the door. After saying my morning St. Michael prayer, I feel an invisible hedge of protection around myself, my house, my family, my friends, and my community. Because I find angels intriguing and inviting, I have recently taken some time to learn more about the other angels and archangels. They are extraordinary angelic beings because they are an extension of God. We can tap into them at any time for their infinite guidance, wisdom, strength, assistance, and power. They are with us all the time, but because of our free will, we may not always feel their presence. They need our permission to intercede in our lives. You might find that, just by reading through their names and descriptions, you form a natural connection or bond with one or two of them. If you do, I encourage you to learn about the angels that resonate with you so you can tap into their divine love, light, powerful healing, and guidance within your own life. They are created by God to assist, guide, and protect us. Let me introduce you to them now.[29] They channel me all the time in conscious and subconscious moments. I am grateful for this gift that I can share with my family, friends, and clients. You must be mindful and respectful of the Angels and be grounded and educated to call them in for the highest good of you and highest good of all. Reach out to a professional for assistance.

Archangel Ariel: Lioness of God

Archangel Ariel is associated with providing us with our physical needs and assists us with environmental issues. She helps us with prosperity and abundance (love, finances, creativity, health, and wealth). She is known as the patron angel of animals. She is associated with the color pale pink, and the crystal associated with this color is rose quartz. This color represents strength of character, dominance, and confidence.

Archangel Azrael: Whom God Helps

Archangel Azrael is associated with bringing departed souls to heaven and helps the grief stricken and grief counselors. He is the patron angel of the clergy. His color is creamy white. The crystal associated with him is yellow calcite. His color represents providing happiness and creates vitality and optimism.

---

[29] . www.summitlighthouse.org/archangels. www.crystalguidance.com/articles/archangels.html

Archangel Chamuel: He Who Sees God

Archangel Chamuel is associated with easing our anxieties and brings about personal and global peace, comfort, and love. He can also help us find lost objects and people. He is the patron angel of personal and global peace and calmness. The colors associated with this angel are pale green and pink, which are associated with virtue, love, and the heart. These colors stand for hope, health, balance, honesty, and love. The crystals associated with this angel are rose quartz and green fluorite.

Archangel Gabriel: Messenger of God

Archangel Gabriel is associated with hope and purity. Together with the seraphim, the angels guard the immaculate concept of the God design for everyone and reinforce the flame of hope around the world. He is the patron angel of writers, teachers, journalists, and anyone in the field of communication. In addition, he is a helper to parents and parents-to-be and is the angel of children. He is associated with the colors white and copper, which represents brilliant perfection, innocence, purity, and immortality. The crystals associated with him are diamond, citrine, and howlite.

Archangel Haniel: Glory of God

Archangel Haniel is associated with helping with clairvoyance. She awakens spiritual intuition and helps release the old and embrace the new. She supports women in healing emotional and physical health issues and assists them during the moon cycles. She is the angel of passion, grace, beauty, and harmony and the patron angel of feminine support. Her color is moonlight blue. The crystal associated with this color is moonstone.

Archangel Jeremiel: Mercy of God

Archangel Jeremiel is associated with helping heal old emotional wounds and forgiveness. He helps with positive changes, can assist you with prophetic visions, and conducts life reviews so adjustments can be made. He is the patron angel of emotional healing. He is associated with the color dark purple, and the crystal associated with this color is amethyst.

Archangel Jophiel: Beauty of God

Archangel Jophiel is associated with wisdom and illumination. She helps us heal negative situations. She is known as the patron of artists and helps bring beauty and organization to homes and offices. She is the angel of patience, wisdom, and illumination and the patron angel of artists. She uplifts thoughts and feelings, and she is associated with pink, which represents love. The crystals associated with archangel Jophiel are pink tourmaline, rose quartz, and rubellite, known to uplift thoughts and feelings and clear clutter out of your life.

Archangel Metatron: God Is Light
(Formerly the prophet Enoch who ascended after living a virtuous life)

Archangel Metatron is associated with helping heal learning disorders and childhood issues. He is known as the angel of life and the angel of the covenant. His name means "one who guards" or "one who serves behind God's throne." He is the patron angel of children. He works with indigo and crystal children and is associated with green with dark pink. He is represented in a number of esoteric systems of knowledge and is believed to be the angel who guards the tree of life and records in the Book of Life, also known as the Akashic records. The crystal associated with his colors is watermelon tourmaline.

Archangel Michael: He Who Is Like God

Archangel Michael is the prince of the archangels and of the angelic hosts. He directs the guardian angels of protection, our guardian angels. He releases us from fear and doubt, provides protection, and clears away any negative energy. He is the angel of courage, strength, and protection and the patron angel of law enforcement and the military. He is associated with the color violet blue (cobalt). Blue represents feelings, fluidity, responsibility, and the power of concentration. The crystals associated with archangel Michael are obsidian and sugilite.

Archangel Raguel: Friend of God

Archangel Raguel is known for bringing harmony to relationships and helps heal misunderstandings. He can help you attract wonderful new friends. He is associated with the color aqua blue; whose associated crystal is aquamarine.

Archangel Raphael: He Who Heals

Archangel Raphael can assist healers and provides healing to the body physically, mentally, emotionally, and spiritually. He is the patron angel of all those in the field of medicine. The color associated with him is emerald green, and the associated crystals are emerald, malachite, and jade.

Archangel Raziel: The Secrets of God

Archangel Raziel heals spiritual and psychic blocks. He has the keys to enable you to tap into divine wisdom in any situation. He helps with understanding the universe, remembering and healing past lives, and understanding esoteric wisdom such as dream interpretation. He is the patron angel of lawmakers and lawyers. The color associated with this archangel is the rainbow. The crystal associated with this color is the clear quartz.

Archangel Sandalphon: Angel of Music and Prayer
(Formerly the prophet Elijah, who ascended after living a virtuous life)

Archangel Sandalphon is known as an angel who cares for the earth and directs the music in heaven. He presents people's prayers to God, inspires them to praise God in creative ways, and helps them use the talents God has given them to contribute to the world. He is the patron angel of music and is associated with the color turquoise. The crystal associated with this color is turquoise, peridot, apache tears, and aqua aura crystals.

Archangel Uriel: God Is Light

Archangel Uriel is known as the angel of wisdom and philosophy. He illuminates our minds with insights and new ideas. He shines the light of God's truth into the shadows of our dark confusion. He is the patron angel of literature and music. The color associated with this angel is yellow, and the associated crystal is amber.

Archangel Zadkiel: Righteousness of God

Archangel Zadkiel is the angel of compassion and forgiveness. He assists in healing memory problems and with other mental functions. He helps remind us of our divine spiritual mission. He is the patron angel of all who forgive. The color associated with this angel is dark indigo blue. The crystal associated with this color is lapis lazuli, which can also assist students while taking tests.

Do not be afraid to open your heart and mind to learning about these angels. They are with you right now and are waiting for you to give them permission to intercede on your behalf in your life. They will give you guidance, wisdom, and direction. All you must do is open your heart. When you do, you will find out how really cool they are. Give them permission by saying, "I give you permission to intercede in my life for my highest good and the highest good of all."

Numbers are a special way that your angels communicate with you. For example, when you look at the clock and see 1:11, 2:22, 3:33, etc., that means your angels are letting you know that they are with you and sending you communication. Look up those angel numbers and read their messages. When you find a feather, that is your angel. You also might see butterflies, dragonflies, eagles, hawks, keys, or a heads-up penny. Your angels will continue to reach out to you. When you are mindful and choose to be in the *now*, you open your awareness and will notice these signs. You will learn how to unravel their messages for your soul journey.

Remember that nothing is an accident. There are no mistakes in life. Be aware of people, places, and circumstances because there are messages for you in these situations. Keep a journal throughout your life and write down your dreams, the numbers that you continually see, and things that ignite and excite you, and this will aid you in mapping out your destiny. Do not get so caught up in all this that you forget to be in the moment of life with your loved ones, family, and friends. It is the personal connections and relationships that help us discover our destiny. Learn to love and embrace each moment and feel that divine love flow through you and wrap around everyone near you. As my dad always said, "It's a beautiful thing."

Please visit my website at www.mindfulblissliving.com to set up your own oracle angel reading.

PART 6

Final Words

Photographed by Natalie M. Morrison

CHAPTER 35

Finding Your Authentic You

As a parent, I am guilty of parenting my children by my own compass. It is the personal gauge that we all use to navigate life. I have been known to attempt to shove my beliefs, views, and opinions down their throats, only to find out that they resented me for it later. I am guilty of trying to, in their eyes, micromanage and navigate their lives because, in my mind, I thought that I was just being helpful and supportive. What I have learned—no, what I am still learning—is that the key is that each person must find his or her own compass.

I do not want any of us, including my own kids, to fall into the trap of being, believing, acting, and doing what our parents or the masses of society expect us to do. I want each person to find his or her own true, authentic, pure self.

What characteristics do you admire about yourself? Whom do you want to emulate and why? What are your God-given strengths, talents, and spiritual gifts? What excites you? I hope that while reading this book, something stirred within your soul—an awakening to a bigger part of your truth that you have yet to discover. I hope that you take the time to ask yourself who you really are and who you want to become. Once you begin to discover and write the answers to that question, you will find yourself on the path to your own self-discovery. When you find your authentic self, you can choose to clear your own ancestral beliefs and baggage which no longer serves you. You are able to leave your mark on this world to make it a better place for yourself and for each generation that follows. Believe in God or whatever you consider your higher power to be and believe in you!

CHAPTER 36

To My Children

My wish for each of you:

- Live life to the fullest and never be afraid to be your true, authentic self.
- Learn to love yourself.
- Forgive yourself and others.
- Laugh and feel the joy of the big and little blessings in life.
- Learn to laugh at yourself.
- Be careful with your words because they can uplift or destroy not only yourself, but also others.
- Be authentic.
- Be courageous.
- Not let others' opinions of you determine your self-worth.
- Know that you are loved, and you are love.
- Be gracious and generous.
- Lend a helping hand to those in need.
- Prepare for a life of longevity.
- Let your handshake equal your integrity.
- Let God be your compass.
- Love what you do and do what you love.
- Keep an open mind for continued growth and learning.

- Travel the world and meet new people.
- Know that you can do, be, and achieve whatever you set your mind to.
- Love and take care of each other.
- Be a great friend.
- Listen twice as much as you speak.
- Know that sometimes silence is the best answer.
- Have gratitude.
- Be hopeful and have humility.
- Be a critical thinker and don't be afraid to ask questions.
- Be dedicated to whatever you are working to achieve.
- Have integrity.
- Possess and exhibit patience and kindness.
- Use your discernment by listening to your inner voice.
- Enjoy the wonders of the world.
- Be understanding with yourself and with others.
- Be truthful with yourself and others.
- Be the love and the light that this world needs.
- Pray to God, Jesus, and your angels; ask them to intercede in your life.
- Be the author of your own story.

I love you all to the moon and back and around the world a thousand times. You are all a part of my life mission, purpose, and passion. You each have played a part in molding me into the person I am today. I hope that these words give you comfort, support, peace, guidance, and love as you make your way out into this great big world.

XOXO, Mom, a.k.a. Smother

CHAPTER 37

Women in My Life Who Matter

Sandra

My mom—what can I say? She is my rock, my love, my believer, my everything! When I was little, hers were the arms that cradled me not only during a bad storm or a disturbing dream but also in my moments of victory. She was my best cheerleader, standing on the sidelines of my life. She always believed in me yet was the first to question me if I veered off the path of my destiny. She gave me the boundaries I needed to be safe but gave me enough space to spread my wings and fly. I cannot ever imagine picking anyone other than her to be my mother on this life journey. Thank you, Mom, for being such a loving, caring, faith-filled mom. Thank you for being such an amazing, nurturing, and wise grandmother to my six children. Thank you for loving my dad, your husband, so unconditionally up until the point of his death in our third-dimensional world and forever, as I know you will, in our eternal, higher, twelve-dimensional world. Thank you for choosing to stay with us on earth after his death to continually provide us with your love, wisdom, faith, and humor to get through life's challenges. Thank you for just being you! I love you with all my heart, body, and soul. For always and forever, you are one of my soul tribe.

Sharon

My grandmother from another mother, Sharon came into my life in my mid-teens. She married my grandfather, Pop-Matt, on my sixteenth birthday. I still remember their wedding, the reception, and the beautiful cake that they bought me. Everyone at the wedding sang me happy birthday. As I got older and after the death of my grandfather, Sharon and I became closer. She has been such a wise owl in my life. She understood things that I was going through, and because she was able to see things from a different angle, she gave me perspectives on life that my mom was too close to see. She completes me. She pours her life, laughter, humor, and light into me and my children. I am forever grateful for this woman because she is the grandmother that I've grown so close to in my adult years. She fills my cup, yet she is so humble that she thanks me for my love. Sharon, you are wiser and stronger than you will ever know. Thank you, God, for giving this woman to me as my grandmother. It's interesting that my paternal grandmother was Elaine (my name), my paternal grandfather was Matthew (my husband's name), and Sharon is also the name of my husband's first wife. It is a triangle of love. God has such a great sense of humor. I love that our lives were woven together.

Marilynn

My mother-in-law, Marilynn, was a little bit intimidating at first because she fiercely protects her clan. So of course, when I began to date her oldest son, she came across as a dragon, which I can appreciate. The more we got to know each other, the more I realized the depth of the love that she has for her tribe, our tribe. She was funny, flamboyant, and full of life, fun, and excitement, like my stepdaughter Ana. She refused to settle for the simple life, and she pushed the envelope and asked questions that others feared asking. These are some of the characteristics that I love about her. She survived the loss of her parents, her sister, and one of her sons. She survived breast cancer, heart and lung surgery, and pancreatic cancer. She is one badass woman, and I am grateful that she is in my corner. I love our long talks about life and her stories of her own youth and that of my husband. I thank her for accepting me for who I am and for loving her son and our six children. We lost my mother-in-law in mid-2020. I will never look at any bird or frog and not think of her. Frogs and birds were her spirit animals. I feel her energy all around our family, and I hear her quiet whispers of guidance, wisdom, direction, and pure love for our family. I miss her desperately every single day. I feel her presence in my windchimes as she sings a melody in the blowing of the wind. I see her presence in the dance of the leaves as the trees release them in the October skies, and like children on a playground in the cool November wind, the leaves tumble and chase one another across the ground. I see her when the moon bounces off its reflection on the ground covered snowy long winter nights. I hear her in the chirping of the birds as spring brings its promise of rebirth and renewal of each year. I feel her loving warmth wrap around me on each sun shiny day. She is forever with me and our family.

CHAPTER 38

Storytelling

Storytelling is one of the oldest forms of communication. It allows the storyteller to connect his or her soul with another's. When you write, you have the ability to see where you were, where you are, and where you are headed. The magic of storytelling is that you can cocreate and write your personal journey. Although you can never unwrite the past, you can use its lessons to create a better tomorrow. History is to be remembered and passed onto future generations for the lessons that need to be learned. We need to take those lessons and the wisdom gained from our history and pave a better path for our world. This path will provide a fresh perspective on life for your current "now" and your future.

As I completed this book, COVID-19 became a 2019–2021 global pandemic. Through this life-shifting global awakening came the destruction and death of many people, businesses, organizations, and institutions. The aftermath also brought with it fear, anger, and chaos, with riots, people fighting people, misunderstandings, polarity, and continued hatred. I hope and pray that I will continually choose to stand in the gap of enlightenment and higher understanding of unconditional love. Racism and inequality still darken our world with their huge shadows of injustice and inhumane acts, but I do believe that most of us are good and hold the light that this world desperately needs. The topic of polarity and dense energy is heavy for most of us to bear, but it has shifted our neighborhoods, communities, states, country, and world into a greater awareness of the changes that need to occur. It's time that we all acknowledge this injustice and stand together in peace and love to ignite the flame of hope for the change our world desperately needs for the healing of ancestral wounds that so many of our brothers and sisters carry. This illumination and realignment will bring us truths and justice for all humanity. No more injustice, untruth, human trafficking, evil, lies, hate, separation, polarity, victim mentality—let us all stand in the truth of *love* and *light* for every living human being!

For some, the pandemic provided an opportunity to reflect. With this reflection came self and community awareness and personal transcendence, with a deepened enlightenment of unity for the love for our world. Mother Earth had a little time to heal. Families were able to spend more time together. Individuals had a quiet timeout from the noise of the world, which allowed for self-reflection. Communities came together to help one another from a safe distance. Those who were considered essential employees, like our medical workers—including my daughter Natalie as a nurse—had the courage to stand on the front line of this assaultive virus and still stand in the gap, saving lives with their bravery and skill. Teachers, like my husband, became more creative in continuing educational opportunities for their students.

Love is the ultimate solution and answer—self-love and love of others.

I wish you all peace, love, reflection, growth, and awareness, and may you find the true light of your authentic self. When you do, share this gift, and let it shine like a bright diamond, glowing and illuminating the darkness within this world.

Since this book began with the story of my father, I feel that it is appropriate to end it with a poem he wrote in his last few months of life.

The Rainbow Promise
Richard S. Turner Sr.

A little rain falls on everyone. The sky gets dark and cloudy. At the end of the storm sometimes a beautiful rainbow forms to let us know that blue, blue skies and sunshine are just around the corner. So never let a storm keep your spirit down. Let your little light shine like there is no tomorrow.

If you put your mind in a place that makes you happy, you can virtually be in that happy place. Let your free spirit soar to your personal heaven where all is peaceful and happy. God has such a place for all of us. He lets us go there whenever we want to.

Put that beautiful sunshine smile on your face, make your heart feel as light as a feather and know that God will make everything alright.

He always does.[30]

We are both the yin and yang of our existence. We all have light and dark within our being. When you focus on the shadows, that is all you will ever see, but when you focus on your light, you will truly find the beauty of your existence. Find gratitude, find love, and find light, and with that you will find your purpose. When you find your purpose, you find your true authentic self.

---

[30] Turner, Richard. May 2011. "Rainbow Promise."

Lightning Source UK Ltd.
Milton Keynes UK
UKHW012150270521
384511UK00007B/650/J